Contents

About the author

Patricia McBride is a writer and independent training consultant, specialising in management and interpersonal skills training. She runs training courses for people applying for jobs.

Patricia is the author of a companion book to this one *Excel at Interviews* and is also the author of:

The EI Advantage – McGraw Hill, 2002

The Emotional Intelligence Activities Pack – Lifetime Careers Publishing, 2004.

Acknowledgements

I would like to thank the following people for giving their time and assistance in writing this book: Doreen Dace, Rachel Dace, Helen Coffey, Rick Leggatt and Debbie Gregory.

Chapter one
Creative job search ideas

You should read this chapter if you:

- can't find the job you want through advertisements or the 'normal' methods

- want to brush up your knowledge of traditional job search methods

- want to widen your chances of finding exactly the right job for you.

By the end of this chapter you should know:

- how and where to find jobs through advertisements, agencies and the internet

- how to use networking, face to face and on the web

- how to write speculative letters to potential employers

- some innovative ideas on how to get noticed

- about advertising yourself on the web.

Going that bit further

It is said that less than half the jobs available at any one time are advertised. A staggering thought. This means that you must be willing to look wider than your newspaper to find just the job for you. In this chapter we explore where to find jobs through both traditional and other routes.

The traditional route – job advertisements

As we have said, by no means all jobs are advertised, but this is still a major way in which organisations recruit staff. So where do you look?

Newspapers

Naturally, your local paper is a good starting point if you want to work locally. Find out what night they advertise jobs, and also check out if any free newspapers carry advertisements.

National papers also advertise jobs. Here is which paper advertises on what day:

Monday

The Guardian – media, creative, sales, marketing, secretarial

Financial Times - junior finance and accountancy to £45,000

Tuesday

The Guardian – academic appointments, research, teaching, TESOL (teaching English to speakers of other languages), further education and senior higher education

The Times – legal

The Sun – all vacancies

Wednesday

The Guardian – senior and executive appointments, finance, health management, housing, regenerations, environmental, social care, criminal justice, management

The Times – PAs (personal assistants)

Thursday

The Sun – all vacancies

The Guardian – science and technology

The Telegraph – all vacancies

The Times – all vacancies

The Express – all vacancies but specialise in retail, engineering, sales, customer services

Daily Mail – all vacancies, mostly sales, retail, engineering and general appointments

Daily Record – all vacancies

Financial Times - senior finance and accountancy over £45K, and non-financial appointments

Independent – all vacancies in 'education and careers' section

Evening News (Scotland) – all vacancies

Daily Mirror – all vacancies – regional editions

Friday

Financial Times – international recruitments (advertised overseas only)

The Scotsman – all vacancies

Saturday

The Guardian – some vacancies from earlier in week repeated

Sunday

The Sunday Telegraph – all vacancies

The Independent on Sunday – general appointments

The Sunday Times – financial, engineering, healthcare, public health, sales and marketing, telecommunications, executive, general

The Express – all vacancies but specialise in retail, engineering, sales and customer services

Mail on Sunday – small selection of financial vacancies in financial section

Sunday Mail (Scotland) – all vacancies

Independent on Sunday – all vacancies

Scotland on Sunday – all vacancies

Sunday Mirror – all vacancies

News of the World – all vacancies

Sunday Times – all vacancies

Remember also to look in professional journals. Libraries hold many copies and you will be able to look up the details of the journal on the web in most cases.

Employment agencies

There are many, many employment agencies which between them hold thousands of jobs that are not advertised. Some agencies are generalists – they hold different types of vacancy, whilst others specialise only in jobs in one particular field. To find where the agencies are for local jobs look in your *Yellow Pages* or similar directories. For work further afield look in professional journals or on the internet for details of relevant agencies.

Jobs on the web

Many organisations now advertise their vacancies on the web. Surfing round the web you will find sites from:

■ employment agencies

■ universities

■ organisations seeking to fill their own vacancies. Organisations are increasingly only advertising on the web as it saves the very high cost of advertising.

■ private CV writing organisations and advice pages

■ professional bodies.

The web has very many sites for looking for jobs. If you don't know any suitable sites I suggest you start by going to www.google.com or www.google.co.uk. If you want to search by locality, type in something like 'Jobs Cambridge' (remember to click on 'pages from the UK'). If you want to search by type of job, type something like 'Jobs Engineering'.

If you are not sure what type of job you want, type in 'Jobs UK' and sites covering a wide variety of jobs will appear in the google list.

Jobs for people with disabilities

If you have a disability, you can also look for jobs on-line. Searching for a few minutes in google I found The British Council of Disabled people, web address – www.bcodp.org.uk/vacancies/index.shtml as well as www.support4learning.org.uk/jobsearch/jobs, a website offering advice on job search issues as well as advertising some vacancies.

You can also get advice about job related matters from the Helpline of the Disability Discrimination Act. Their contact details are telephone number 0800 882200, textphone 0800 243355. Their website is www.disability.gov.uk and their address is Disability Unit, Department for Work and Pensions, Level 6, Adelphi, 1-11 John Adam Street, London WC2N 6HT. Email: feedback-disability@dwp.gsi.gov.uk

Professional journals

Do remember that many vacancies are advertised in professional journals. You can find many of these in your main library. Alternatively, contact the journal and ask how you can subscribe or if they have a web page showing appointments.

Your college or workers who already work in the field should be able to tell you the names of suitable journals. If you can't find one, you could look in a writers' book called the *Writers & Artists Yearbook* – you'll find one in your main library. They list details of the bigger journals.

Later chapters in this book tell you how to apply for jobs that are advertised, so for now let's concentrate on less traditional routes to finding that perfect job.

Networking – what it is, how to do it

One way to find out about unadvertised jobs is called 'networking'. Networking is simply using (in the nicest possible sense) people you know, and people they know, to discover what opportunities are available.

Even better, these people may be able to recommend you to the shortlister and so help you bypass many other people who are also looking for jobs. Your objective is to get to meet the people who are the decision-makers about filling posts.

Whenever you speak to people, consider them as possible sources of information about job opportunities. This is true whether you are speaking to friends, family, family friends, other students, tutors, neighbours or whoever. Many of them will be in paid employment. They will know, or can find out, what job openings there may be in their organisations.

Alternatively, they may be friends with people who are knowledgeable about other companies, and this can be just as useful.

When you first think about it, speaking about job opportunities to people you know directly may be embarrassing. But remember that the 'old boys' network' has been making life smooth for the people in it for centuries.

Furthermore, many employers appreciate knowing someone who can fill a post. It saves them the trouble and expense of advertising.

Networking – getting started

Write yourself a plan of action. Begin with ten possible contacts. These can be people you know or know of. (Some of your contacts may be through the web – more about that later in this chapter). Ask yourself these questions: 'How will I get in touch with these people?', 'What will I say?'. Remember, these people may not be in a position to offer you a job themselves, but they should be able to give you other contacts and tips on how best to approach them. They may also be able to put in a word for you, give you up-to-date job market information, suggest ideas you've overlooked or ways to improve your presentation skills. Ask them if you can use their name when making an approach, as that can be a good way to introduce yourself.

A good idea is to set yourself a goal that each of these ten people will put you in touch with at least two other people. Continue like this and you will see that you can quickly get to contact a huge number of people. Some contacts will be easy – you'll actually meet the person through your everyday life.

Start with the friendliest person – this will give you more confidence to go on to other more difficult contacts. Here's an example. You've heard a bit about the company your Aunt Jane works for, and just wonder whether there may be some openings...

You

'Aunt Jane, you know that I'm job hunting at the moment. Well, I wonder if you could help me. Your company takes on people to do the sort of work I'm interested in. Do you think you could give me the names of a couple of contacts there who I could speak to about vacancies?'

Aunt Jane

'Sure. You'd need to speak to the head of my department or else the Human Resources Manager. I can give you their names.'

You

'Thanks. If you could warn them I'll be phoning, and put in a good word, that would be really good too. Do you know any people in other companies I could contact?'

With a number of such conversations, you'll start gaining quite a lot of information, so it's important to be organised. Use a card index system or similar (anything that works for you) to keep details of the contacts and what you find out. Here is a card format you may like to use:

Name	Job Title
Organisation	How contact made
Contact details	
Possible vacancies	Contact date
Additional information	Follow up action.

Complete your card every time you contact someone. And file the forms in alphabetical order under the name of the organisation so you can easily find it again.

Sound positive

Each time you speak to a contact – even if it's not actually the person who may be able to offer you the job – sound positive and professional. Be prepared at all times to talk about your skills and strengths – you never know what information may be passed on to the decision maker.

Telephone contacts

Before you pick up the phone, rehearse what you are going to say. If you are likely to get nervous, jot down the key points on a piece of paper to prompt you. Here are some tips for using the telephone:

- choose a phone in a quiet location

- if using a payphone, have plenty of change available or use a phone-card

- sit or stand up straight and smile as you say hello (your posture and facial expressions alter the way your voice sounds – you can *hear* a smile)

- address the person by name

- explain the reason for your call

- mention the name of your contact

- ask if it's a good time to call – offer to call another time if necessary

- have your discussion (see below for typical questions to ask)

- be polite and professional at all times

- try to arrange a meeting to get further information and advice

- if you can't arrange a meeting and they can't help at this time ask their permission to call back in a few weeks to ask again

- thank the person for their time

- write down the results of your contact on your index card.

Questions to ask

If you are successful and your contact gives you some time to discuss a potential vacancy (even if none exists at present), have a few questions in mind. These might include the following.

- What does the job involve?

- What type of person are you looking for?

- Who would be the line manager or supervisor?

- What is a typical working day/week like?

- What induction training is available?

- What continuing training is offered?

- What careers paths would be possible?

- What are the current and future issues for that organisation/ business sector?

- What type of qualifications would help me to get a job in that organisation?

- What particular skills are you looking for?

- What is the best way to obtain these skills without currently being employed by the organisation?

- How can I be informed of vacancies as soon as they occur?

Following through

When you make a contact, always follow up with a polite letter thanking the person for their time and telling them if you have followed up any advice or contacts they gave you. This need only be a short letter, but it is common courtesy and another way of being remembered which may be important in future.

Arranging a meeting

There will come the time when you get to speak to the decision-maker.

He or she may be the personnel manager or head of department. Whether on the phone, or speaking face to face, you will have to judge whether or not it is appropriate to have a lengthy discussion about any vacancies. If the person is willing but doesn't have time at that moment, try to arrange a time to meet or phone when they're less busy.

Take the phone conversation below. You sense that the person you're calling is busy, so this is how you tackle it:

You

'Hello Mr Patel. My name is Amy Thomas. Dorothy Edwards suggested I contact you for a chat about job possibilities. Is this a good time to talk or can I arrange to call back another time?'

Mr Patel

'Dorothy told me you might call. I can spare you a few minutes.'

You

'Thanks very much. I know that you're not advertising for a customer service clerk at the moment, but this is the type of work I'm really interested in and I wondered if there were likely to be any vacancies.'

Mr Patel

'Not as far as I know.'

You

'Well, one reason I'm phoning you in particular is because I know quite a bit about your company from Mrs Edwards and of course from your products. Even though you don't have any vacancies just now, would it be possible for me to take up 20 minutes of your time one day to discuss how I can be in the best position for getting a job with you when one comes up?'

Mr Patel

'Well, I'm really busy, but … well, okay. What about the 14th at 3.30? I'll pencil you in for 30 minutes.'

You

'Thank you so much. I'll look forward to meeting you then.'

The trick here was to persevere without sounding pushy. But however well rehearsed you are, the answer can sometimes be a clear 'no'. In this case, thank the person politely and ask if you could contact them again in a few weeks time if you're still looking for a job. Also ask if they could suggest someone else you could speak to in your search for a job.

If you succeed in arranging a meeting, then well done! Prepare for it well. Although this is not a job interview it is important to take the meeting seriously. Plan ahead what you are going to say and what you want to get from the meeting. Dress smartly and arrive punctually.

Give the contact person an overview of yourself, your career history (if any) and your skills. What you say may begin something like this:

You

'Thank you for seeing me, Ms Holmes. I know that you don't have any clerical vacancies at the moment but as you know I'd be very interested in applying when one comes up. If I tell you a bit about myself you may be able to give me some advice about any other skills or qualifications I might need.

I've just completed City & Guilds in Business Administration. I got good marks for all my coursework and my placement with Jones Insurance went very well. In fact Mrs Dawes there gave me a reference and I've brought a copy along for you. I feel pretty confident I have a good grasp of the skills you need and I'm a very enthusiastic and hard worker. I learn fast too…'

When you feel you've said enough, you may be asked some further questions about yourself. In turn, ask about the company a bit more, what kind of people they look for as employees, advice on what additional experience you should gain to hold you in good stead. See if they can suggest anyone else you can contact in your job search. Do remember to thank the person for the time and follow up the meeting with a polite thank you letter. Remember to record your meeting on your contact card for future reference.

Networking on the web

Web networking has much in common with other networking. One big disadvantage though is that you won't be able to impress people with your charm or the power of your voice. It's important therefore to make the web work best for you. Here are a few tips:

- write grammatically

- keep your writing focussed – be clear about what you want from the other person (and what you can offer in return if there is anything)

- act respectfully towards others at all times, value the time and effort they have put into communicating with you

- give yourself time to build up your network, don't leave it until your studies are almost over or you're out of a job.

Like any networking, work from a position of strength. That works best when you are currently employed or still a student. If you are unemployed, try to undertake temporary or voluntary work so that you look more appealing to those you contact. It doesn't matter if the work is part-time – the other person won't know that.

Where to network online

The most obvious answer is with people whose email address you know. Keep in touch with people who may be in a position to help, and think about what you may be able to offer them in return. Ask your email contacts if they can suggest anyone else you can contact.

There are thousands of discussion groups so you'll be sure to find one in your interest area – and if you can't you can always start one... Through discussion groups you can be in touch with literally dozens of people in no time. You may even get in touch with people who work for your target companies. Remember that your conversations will be public, so be polite, professional and confident at all times.

Remember safety guidelines at all times when communicating with someone on the web. Do not arrange to meet anyone without first telling a parent or an adult you know and trust.

You might also like to look on www.jobsearch.about.com/mpchat.html

USENET

USENET is a compilation of newsgroups resembling electronic bulletin board systems. Businesses list job openings on a relevant newsgroup, although currently many of the vacancies are in the computer field.

Writing 'on spec'

An often overlooked way to find a job is simply to write to an organisation and ask if they've got one. This is known as writing speculatively, more commonly known as 'on spec'. If you can't find a contact and no job is currently being advertised, this can be very worthwhile. Many organisations keep such letters (which should be sent to them with a copy of your CV) on file. This saves them advertising when a vacancy occurs; they simply contact all the people who have sent in details.

Take this example. If you want to get into hotel management, you could write to all the big hotel chains – and indeed your local hotels – asking what openings they have. You have nothing to lose but a little time and a few stamps. You might gain a lot.

If you are writing 'on spec', be clear about what sort of job you seek, or say if you are willing to consider anything they might have to offer. If you are looking for a particular type of work, write the letter very much with that in mind. There is an example overleaf.

Be polite, but don't be overly humble or the reader may not believe you have the confidence and experience to do the job.

As you will see later in this chapter, it is useful to follow up on speculative letters with a phone call. In practical terms, this means that you shouldn't send off more letters than you can follow up. If you realistically couldn't make more than say 15 phone calls a week, then limit your letters to that number if you really want to maximise your chances.

Targeted 'on spec' letters

An alternative way to write 'on spec' letters is to target them to a particular organisation as a response to something you know about the company.

James Potter
33 Church Street
Oldham
OL3 4RR

Mrs S Smith
Big Inn
23-45 High Street
Oldham
OL4 4RE

(today's date)

Dear Mrs Smith

Secretarial vacancies

I am writing to ask if you have any secretarial or clerical vacancies at the moment. As you will see from my enclosed CV, I am just about to leave Blackdown College and have completed an NVQ level 2 in Administration. This has given me some very relevant skills including:

- typing 40 wpm

- knowledge of general office procedures

- ability to use Word, Excel and Powerpoint.

I did a work placement at Dublin Manufacturers and Mr Bower, the Office Manager, has given me a reference which I enclose. As you will see, he found me enthusiastic, quick to learn and flexible.

Working for your company particularly interests me because it has an excellent reputation for being ahead of the field and I feel sure that I could make a positive contribution to your work.

If you have no vacancies at present, I should be very grateful if you could keep my details on file and let me know when one occurs.

Yours sincerely

James Potter

This could be an article you have seen in a newspaper or trade or professional magazine, or something you have learnt about by word of mouth. Here are a few beginnings of such letters to demonstrate the point:

Dear Mr Thomas

I read with interest in this week's Daily Telegraph that your company has just won a big contract to supply Hokomoto with parts for their engines. It occurs to me that in the light of your increased workload you may be looking for more administrative staff. I am…

or

Dear Ms Cohen

This week's Hotels Monthly mentions that you are planning to open a hotel in my area within the next three months. I have recently finished…

or

Dear Miss Schultz

Now that the housing market is finally picking up I am writing to ask whether you anticipate taking on any additional staff. I am…

or

Dear Mr Briggs

This week's Bloxford Recorder mentioned that your company is planning to expand into other areas of the fashion industry. I am…

By responding to changes in the circumstances of an organisation, you will be showing that you have your ear to the ground, and have read the right newspapers and journals. This shows considerable initiative and would impress most potential employers.

Follow-up calls

Whichever type of 'on spec' letter you send, do follow it up with a phone call a few days later. Have your letter at hand and ask to speak to the person to whom you wrote. Introduce yourself, explain why you're ringing, and find out whether it is a convenient time to talk. Your aim is to get the person's response to your letter. If it is positive, ask if you can meet to discuss it further, or whether you should complete an application form. If it isn't, then all is not lost. You can ask for your details to be kept on file.

If the person hasn't had time to read the letter, ask when it would be convenient to call back. Thank them for their time, and if you are using networking techniques described earlier in this chapter, record your call in your card index or other system.

One student I know was looking for part-time work to supplement her grant and wrote to 12 local restaurants asking if they had suitable vacancies. Within three months eight of the restaurants phoned back asking to see her!

Blowing all the rules

If you are really desperate, and have tried everything else and failed, or if you seek work in a creative field and are exceptionally original, consider breaking all the rules in this book! Maybe you can write a covering letter that will make you stand out by its sheer originality and creativity. Try to link it to the type of work you want to do.

- Want to work in publishing?
  Design yourself a book cover with your details on the back!

(Think of an original and meaningful title for the book *'Job Search Techniques'* by (your name), *'Seeking Success'* by (your name) and so on)

- Want to work in advertising?
  Write an advertisement for yourself

- Want to work in graphic design?
  Design a poster telling about yourself

- Want to work in fabric design?
  Send a sample of fabric you've made, perhaps incorporating your name

- Want to work in computing?
  Design a web page for yourself and send a copy of the home page and the net address

You might even like to consider going really crazy and drawing a cartoon CV. Whilst this sort of CV may not be conventional, many employers would be curious about someone who could so cleverly tell you so much about themselves. I saw a really excellent cartoon CV, and the author always got offered an interview.

Here's a real life story about two young men who decided to take an alternative approach.

David and Michael had just finished college and wanted to get into the advertising business in the middle of the longest recession Britain had known since the 1930s. The advertising industry was in a bad way. Staff were being laid off rather than being taken on. Very, very few jobs were advertised and they didn't even manage to get an interview for those few jobs they could find to apply for.

Things were desperate. But they were determined. This is what they did.

They found the names of 23 advertising agencies in their area and identified the name of the key person to approach in each agency (all were men). Jon and Michael then bought some pink scented writing paper and envelopes and a green pen. As well as the usual address on the front of each envelope they wrote 'PERSONAL' in big letters. They tried to make the handwriting look feminine. This ensured that Mr Big's secretary wouldn't open the letter and that it would be opened directly by Mr Big himself.

Inside they placed a photo of themselves taken in a photo booth. They were informal photos in which they tried to look like brothers on a day out. The letter (again on pink paper written in green ink) was along the lines of:

'Dear Mr ……..

'I don't know if you remember that evening in a Brighton car park 22 years ago, but our mother Janie certainly remembers you."

(They'd got his attention by now!) From there they managed to turn the letter into a funny plea for an interview for a job. Of the 23 agencies they approached, 22 offered them interviews and four offered jobs…

Why was this approach successful? Remember – they were looking for jobs in a creative industry. Their approach was very creative. Any potential employer would be sensible enough to think, 'If they can be this creative to get to see me they'll also be creative working for me.'

For more details of writing a covering letter to include with your CV see Chapter eleven.

The web as a marketing tool

Web marketing is not for novices as designing a web page can be tricky. However, it is a growing trend and is of obvious benefit if you are in the IT world. It would be unwise to rely solely on this method of job search unless you are in an industry where this is the norm. See it as an additional tool to use alongside traditional methods if it is right for you. When you are applying for jobs remember to send your web address and also consider sending some pages with your CV or application form if appropriate. You could certainly take them with you to the interview.

It follows that you must take as much care with your web page design as you would with any other job search method. A poor web page is unlikely to get any prospective employer picking up the phone or e-mailing you in response. For that reason, only attempt a page if you are sure you can do a good job or get someone else to design one for you.

Advantages of a web page

Increasingly common, web page self marketing is a real bonus. Many employers are competent on the internet and you can include details of your web page in any information you send them. They'll be impressed! Other advantages are that you can show samples of your work on your web pages – this is your web portfolio. The site itself will also demonstrate your skills and you can show that you are very up to date.

Some dos and don'ts

Do make sure that:

- your web page is up and running before you give the address to prospective employers

- everything on your website is professional, from your CV to the graphics

- your site works – all links do just that

- your website is coherent – that it sticks to one theme so that prospective employers are clear what you're offering

- you make separate links for each section of your web page. Remember to put all these links on your opening page. Links might include your CV, testimonials, references, and sample of your work.

- you use both graphics and text.

Don't:

- include a copy of your photograph – employers could be open to charges of discrimination

- include irrelevant information.

What to include

There are no hard and fast rules about web design for job search. This means that you have a free hand to show your creativity. And if you're not sure what to include, look for examples already existing on the web for inspiration.

Books on website design

There are many books on this topic now. You might like to look at the 'Dummies' range – they're always easy to follow and pleasant to read.

Buying web building expertise

Maybe you've decided to pay someone to design a web page for you. To find someone reliable, you could start in no better place than on the web. Look for designers whose work you like. If you can't tell who designed a web page, the information may be 'hidden' at the top of the home page. Most browsers have a 'View Source' or 'View HTML' option and it may reveal the designer's name.

Alternatively, ask around; a personal reference is often best. Make sure you get a quote before you start and that you're happy that the designer can meet your deadline. Another tip; remember that your web page may need updating regularly. If this is true for you, don't ask a college friend who may vanish when the course ends.

Useful organisations for jobseekers with disabilities

This is just a selection of the many organisations which will be able to help you.

Coverdale Organisation plc

Runs a Leadership Development Programme and offers training to disabled people who want to develop their management and teamwork skills.

The Coverdale Organisation Ltd – Plestowes Barn, Hareway Lane, Barford, Warwick CV35 8DD. Tel: 01926 625757. Fax 01926 625758. www..coverdale.co.uk Email: web.enquiry@coverdale.co.uk

Disability Action (Northern Ireland)

Offers information and support for people with disabilities.

Head Office – Belfast, Portside Business Park, 189 Airport Road West, Belfast BT3 9ED. Tel : 028 9029 7880. Text : 028 9029 7882. Fax : 028 9064 5779. www.disabilityaction.org email: hq@disabilityaction.org

Employers Forum on Disability

National network of employers who seek to develop their policies and practice on employing people with disabilities. Whilst they don't operate a placement service, they can provide member details.

Employers' Forum on Disability – Nutmeg House, 60 Gainsford Street, London SE1 2NY. Tel: 020 7403 3020. Fax: 020 7403 0404. Minicom: 020 7403 0040. Email: website.enquiries@employers-forum.co.uk

Employment Opportunities for People with Disabilities

This organisation aims to help people with disabilities break down barriers of disability and find employment. Services available include

Job Clubs, help with identifying abilities, writing CVs and job applications, preparing for interview and obtaining aims and equipment.

Employment Opportunities – 123 Minories, London EC3N 1NT. Tel: 020 7481 2727. Fax: 020 7481 9797. Minicom: 020 7481 2727. Email: info@employmentopportunities.org.uk   www.opportunities.org.uk

The Papworth Trust

Papworth Employment Programmes support disabled people getting into, and staying in, paid employment. Their activities include:

- supported placement scheme
- worklink
- work preparation
- vocational assessments

- fast track
- job coaching
- rehabilitation pogramme
- disability awareness training

Papworth Trust – Papworth Everard, Cambridge CB3 8RG. Tel: 01480 830341. Fax 01480 831919. www.papworth.org.uk
Email: info@papworth.org.uk

Shaw Trust

Enables people with disabilities and mental health problems to maximise their potential work opportunities.

Shaw Trust Information Resource – Shaw House, Epsom Square, White Horse Business Park, Trowbridge, Wiltshire BA14 0XJ. Tel: 01225 716350. Fax: 01225 716334. Minicom: 08457 697288. www.shaw-trust.org.uk
Email: stir@shaw-trust.org.uk

Chapter checklist

To job search creatively you should:

- look at advertisements in newspaper, journals and magazines
- ask employers if you can see their internal jobs advertising list
- contact employment agencies
- contact your Jobcentre/Jobcentre Plus or Connexions/careers centre

- network – use contacts to find out details of people who may be able to help you with your job search. These contacts can be personal or via the internet.

- use vacancies chatrooms, web forums and mailing lists to increase your chances of networking effectively. Remember when using chatlines to follow safety advice and don't arrange to meet anyone without warning your parents or an adult you know and trust.

- use your contacts both for details of jobs and advice on how best to present yourself

- always prepare yourself in advance for either a face to face or telephone conversation with a contact

- make sure you thank your contact for spending time talking to you

- follow up a contact with a thank you letter

- if your contact can't help, ask if s/he knows any other possible contact

- have a system for recording your contacts

- write 'on spec' to organisations you'd like to work for, enclosing your CV

- write to organisations in the news (unless it's for redundancies!) – they may be taking on more staff

- be positive, remembering that you are worth employing

- think of creative ways to get yourself noticed

- consider using a web page to market yourself.

Chapter two
How to please a shortlister

You should read this chapter:

- before you begin to complete your application form or write your CV.

By the end of the chapter you should know:

- the mechanisms which shortlisters use to select candidates for interview

- some tips for making it easy for shortlisters to select you for interview.

Think like a shortlister

When you are completing your application form or writing a CV for a job, it is really helpful to know how managers shortlist. By doing this, you can anticipate what they are looking for and make sure you provide it.

In large organisations there is often a personnel or human resource specialist who guides managers through the recruitment process. Either alone, or with the manager, they will select which of the potential applicants gets shortlisted for interview.

However it is true that in many organisations there is no one with specialist knowledge of recruitment and many shortlisters are not trained. This means they may not follow the procedures in this chapter. But take heart. By following these guidelines you will still give yourself the best chance of being shortlisted.

What follows is how good shortlisters operate. It can't take into account the individual peculiarities of untrained people. Increasingly though organisations are using procedures such as those described in this chapter because it can save them from being seen as unfair and perhaps taken to an industrial tribunal. They will often keep the notes on how they short-listed and on the interview for six months in case of later challenges.

By the way, this means that if you are not shortlisted when you expected to be, you could contact the organisation and ask why. This may be useful information to help you when you apply for your next job.

Job descriptions and person specifications

When managers are shortlisting, they base their choice on how your information matches the items in the job description and the person specification for that job. Some organisations call the personal specification 'competencies'.

Chapter eight – *Dazzling CVs* explains in more detail the difference between the two. But briefly, a job description describes the tasks the person has to do and a person specification (or competencies) describes the person who could do those tasks. For example, the task on the job description could be 'type manager's letters' and the corresponding item on the person specification could be 'able to type at 45 wpm'. Sometimes items in the person specification will have 'essential' or 'desirable' written beside them.

So when shortlisters are reading through a pile of application forms or CVs, their task is quite mechanical. They are looking for someone who has the skills, personality and abilities identified to do the job well – in other words to meet the criteria they set. Some employers concentrate on both the job description and the person specification to help them do this, others rely much more heavily on the person specification. They will look first at the 'essential' items as these are the most important. Often they shortlist from what you said about those items. If necessary, they will also look at the 'desirable' items to help them make a decision.

To make sure you get shortlisted it is therefore important to look at both documents if they are provided. If they are not, look at Chapter eight which shows you how to work out what would be in them if you had them.

To help managers shortlist they will have a grid something like this:

Candidate's name			
Job description items	**Met**	**Partly met**	**Not met**
Type manager's correspondence			
Deal with callers to the office			
Answer the telephone			
Deal with customer queries			
Keep the office tidy and file all documents accurately			

Sometimes they may use numbers:

Candidate's name		
Scoring 1 = Not mentioned, 2 = Poor match, 3 = Good match, 4 = Exceptional match		
Person specification items		**Score**
Able to type at 45wpm	E*	
Customer service skills	E	
Telephone answering skills	D	
Experienced at filing	D	
Organised/good timekeeper	E	

*E indicates essential, D indicates desirable

As they read through your information, they simply tick one of the boxes or decide a score. The people with the highest score or most ticks in the 'met' or 'partly met' boxes get shortlisted.

This means that you should always present information about yourself in the same order as is shown in the job description and person specification. Make it easy for the shortlister to choose you. Chapter eight shows you in more detail how to do this.

Activity

Look at an advertisement for a job that interests you. Alternatively, phone the organisation for a job description and person specification. Now think about the skills, knowledge and attributes you could offer the employer. Imagine that you are shortlisting. How many of the items mentioned could you meet to gain a 'met' or 'partly met' mark?

Tip – don't be put off because you can't meet all the items. Even if you can only meet some, go for the job if you really want it – others will be in the same position as yourself. What have you got to lose?

Chapter checklist

Shortlisters who are trained will follow good practice when selecting candidates for interview. They will:

- use the job description and person specification or sometimes the person specification alone as the basis for their selection

- have designed a selection grid to cover the items on these documents, or sometimes only the items on the person specification

- use the grid to help them decide who to invite to interview. They do this by checking the items on the grid against the information provided on the CV or application form

- concentrate more on those items marked 'essential' than those marked 'desirable'

- keep the documents for six months in case of queries from candidates.

Chapter three
Self analysis

You should read this chapter:

■ before you begin to complete an application form or write a CV.

By the end of this chapter you should know:

■ how to analyse your skills, experience, likes and dislikes

■ where to turn to for help with this analysis

■ how to sell your leisure activities

■ how to use words in a winning way.

Your goal

No employer would take on a new member of staff without interviewing them first. And many colleges interview prospective students too, rather than selecting them purely on the basis of their grades and application forms. When you present yourself on paper in the form of a CV or an application form what you are trying to do is to sell yourself. This means that, generally speaking, *your goal in presenting yourself on paper is to get an interview.* All the information in this chapter is equally valuable for college or job applications as well as for compiling a CV.

Self analysis

So, let's have a good look at this product you have to sell – you! Imagine for a moment a person who has to interview candidates for a job or college place. He or she is looking to 'buy' (or select for interview) the best possible person. Unless they happen to know any candidate each person, at this stage, is simply a collection of facts. Initially the shortlister will be looking for some basic requirements. These are a) what you can offer, b) your strengths, c) your weak points and d) your attributes and how they match the job they have to offer.

Researching the shortlister

When you analyse yourself, always have the shortlister in mind. Keep asking yourself: 'What will most impress the person who reads my application form or CV?' Thinking like this will help you to keep focused on the main purpose of the task – to get an interview.

If possible, try to find out who may read your form or CV. A college lecturer, head of department, human resource manager? Put yourself in that person's shoes. Remember, whoever it is will be looking for *relevance* in your information to the course or job in question.

My skills

Let's start your self-analysis on a positive note – your good qualities. This is probably, in fact, the most difficult place for you to start because most people are far more ready to own up to their failings. However, it's got to be done and, rather like taking medicine, you feel good afterwards even if you cringe at the time. Once you've read the lists of skills-related words or statements it's a good idea for you to make notes of those which apply to you. You will find further suggestions to write in your notebook as you work through this book.

In your notebook, write a list of everything you can do. Things you can do are your skills, you don't have to be perfect at them, just reasonably competent. What follows are categories of skills as a prompt – you will probably be able to add to them. To help you to remember all your skills (you may not have used all of them recently or consciously thought about them as skills), make a list of as many different tasks you have completed as possible. For example, did you undertake any project at college or school that required skills not usually used? What skills have you used for studying or jobs you have done? What skills have you developed just from being with people or from helping around the house or with children?

Communication skills

- listening well
- teaching others
- speaking in groups
- writing legibly
- translating
- defending yourself verbally
- writing concisely
- proofreading accurately

- communicating clearly
- speaking clearly
- calming others
- explaining complicated ideas
- writing analytically
- having clear, easy to read handwriting
- putting across an opposing viewpoint

Practical skills

- fixing cars
- keyboarding
- carpentry
- cooking
- laying bricks
- sewing
- using a computer
- metalwork
- knitting

- filing
- driving
- first aid
- riding a bike
- plastering
- swimming
- painting
- demonstrating

Financial skills

- budgeting
- calculating
- understanding the banking system
- paying bills
- evaluating
- analysing

People skills

- caring for disadvantaged people
- speaking in groups
- being empathetic
- advising
- team-building
- motivating
- mentoring
- co-operating
- challenging
- leading
- organising
- supporting others
- liaising
- counselling

Creative skills

- drawing
- designing
- painting
- decorating
- inventing
- photography
- modelling
- developing
- document layout
- producing
- singing
- dancing
- composing
- choreographing
- acting
- playing an instrument
- writing creatively
- web designing

Thinking skills

- editing
- analysing
- planning
- programming
- sorting
- devising
- designing
- preparing
- scheming
- shaping
- formulating

- originating
- conceiving
- imagining
- investigating
- researching
- enquiring
- questioning
- examining
- exploring
- inspecting

Activity: SWOT

Spend a few minutes undertaking a SWOT analysis of your skills. SWOT is a mnemonic for Strengths, Weaknesses, Opportunities and Threats. This type of analysis can be useful for all sort of decision making.

Strengths (What I'm good at)	**Weaknesses** (Skills I'd like to be better at)
Opportunities (to use my strengths and overcome my weaknesses)	**Threats** (to using my strengths and overcoming weaknesses)

My personality

Once you have listed your skills, you need to consider positive aspects of your personality. This is increasingly important because recent research has shown that something called emotional intelligence is much more significant than skills or qualifications when it comes to being an achiever. Daniel Goleman, author of *Working with Emotional Intelligence* (published by Bloomsbury, 1998) defines it as acting in a mature, considered fashion and being independent, working well with others, understanding yourself and having empathy with others. It also means being able to control your moods, motivate yourself and having good communication skills.

So what positive personality aspects can you offer? Head up another sheet of paper in your notebook or a new file on your PC and list all the words that describe your personality. It is hard for some people to apply positive adjectives to their personality so you might like to try the following exercise.

Activity

Imagine that you are your best friend (or indeed a doting relative). He or she meets someone who explains that they have a vacancy for a job that sounds just right for you. They decide to strike while the iron's hot and do a selling job on your behalf. What would they say to the other person? How would they describe you? What skills would they highlight? What positive personal qualities would they mention? See the prompt list below for ideas.

Note those qualities that apply to you and then add to them as necessary:

- kind
- sympathetic
- helpful
- consistent
- happy
- determined

- thoughtful
- empathetic
- diligent
- reliable
- humorous
- assertive

- strong-minded
- willing to learn
- caring
- patient
- adaptable
- persistent
- resolute
- courageous
- adventurous
- sharp-witted
- resourceful
- lively
- academic
- observant
- mature
- careful
- glamorous
- sophisticated
- methodical
- elegant
- energetic
- bold
- dynamic
- imaginative
- charitable

- flexible
- open-minded
- supportive
- honest
- responsible
- obliging
- cheerful
- considerate
- intelligent
- capable
- active
- quick-witted
- charismatic
- charming
- tenacious
- circumspect
- smart
- tidy
- fair
- stable
- modest
- co-operative
- straightforward
- creative
- perceptive

- self-controlled
- innovative
- optimistic
- team worker
- conscientious
- committed
- self-aware
- self-motivated.

My experience to date

Your list of 'experience' should to some extent overlap with your list of skills. If you are thinking 'what experience?', remember all the different things you have done. What jobs have you had? Have you:

- done any voluntary work, even informally
- undertaken work shadowing
- had special responsibility at school or college
- had special responsibilities at home
- travelled
- had responsibilities as a member of a club
- done something unusual?

All of these experiences will have provided you with something relevant to offer an employer or college, if only something to talk about at interview (but more on that later).

Let's look at two quite different examples. For the first, let's assume that you had some work experience for two weeks as a receptionist in a hotel. Most receptionist jobs involve attending to guests, checking guests in and out, answering the phone and making bookings.

Receptionists may also undertake other office work, e.g. typing. If we break down these examples we see that each has required more skills than was immediately obvious.

Attending to guests requires you to:

- have good communication skills
- work with members of the public

- be courteous

- be patient

- be able to respond to queries, perhaps at short notice

- be able to cope with crises (double booking, people getting ill, etc)

- keep calm.

Checking residents in and out requires you to:

- be methodical

- write legibly or make entries into the computer correctly

- communicate clearly

- respond to queries

- handle cash, credit cards, etc.

Answering the phone requires you to:

- have a good telephone manner

- take accurate messages

- respond effectively to the caller

- put calls through to the correct extension

- be efficient.

By looking at your experience in this way, you may also discover some skills you hadn't thought of before. Remember, a skill is simply something you can do. For example, it is a real skill to handle crisis situations effectively and not everyone can be pleasant with awkward customers for eight hours at a stretch.

A second example might be newspaper delivery. On one level it seems a fairly humble occupation; after all, quite young adults take on this job. However, let's analyse the skills and personal qualities involved.

Newspaper delivery involves:

- being prompt and reliable

- being able to work unsupervised
- being efficient – delivering the right paper to the right house
- being honest
- being polite to customers.

My likes and dislikes

You probably have enough experience of the world of work to know a bit about what you like and dislike. Think about any jobs, work experience or voluntary work (even unofficial) you have done. What did you enjoy? What excited you? What left you feeling bored? What did you positively hate? This type of analysis will not only help you to select a job but also to sell yourself enthusiastically about those topics you enjoy.

Getting help with your analysis

Undertaking an analysis of your positive points can be a difficult task. For this reason you may like to think about getting help from others. Obviously, you need to ask people you can trust and who will give you an honest answer. Also, it makes sense to ask more than one person. Choose people who see you in different circumstances – a friend you socialise with would not see you in the same way as a teacher or employer for example. Don't take everything people say at face value – really think about their comments. Do you agree with them? What examples could you give to back up the qualities or skills they have highlighted?

Using your Progress File: Achievement planner

Most students have a Progress File: Achievement planner (or Record of Achievement) which documents their academic and personal progress throughout their school career. If you have either of these, you should find plenty of things to use when writing CVs or completing application forms. You may be able to use it to think about your skill and personal development throughout the years – particularly in areas relevant to the job or course you are applying for. Chapters six and seven show you how to record this information effectively.

Selling your leisure interests

So, how does identifying and recording your leisure interests help you with the application process? To answer this, let's look at university and job applications separately for a minute, then we'll look at ways in which you can write this section most effectively.

> *'One applicant had written under 'Leisure interests', 'My main hobby is completing application forms.' It made me laugh at the time but then I started thinking that this person might be too flippant. Not only that, but the comment seemed to imply he'd been applying for dozens of jobs. Why hadn't he been getting them?'*

> **Quote from an employer**

University applications

The UCAS application form does not specifically ask about leisure interests, although these could be included in the 'Personal Statement' section. Chapter six gives you advice on how to complete this.

Job applications and CVs

Most application forms have a section headed 'Leisure interests' or something similar. If, however, there is no such heading and you particularly want to tell the organisation about a leisure interest that is relevant to the job, you can always mention this in the covering letter you send with your form (Chapter ten covers this in more detail).

Likewise, most people include a section in their CVs headed 'Leisure interests' or 'Additional information'.

> *'One applicant for a job as community care assistant said, 'I like to knit and sew and yes, I even enjoy ironing.' I suppose she thought that she would be an old-fashioned home help but the job has changed a lot. To me this said that this person did not read the job description carefully enough.'*

> **Quote from a local authority employer**

Presenting leisure interests

For many people, finding something to say under this section is really difficult. You think to yourself, 'Well, all I do is watch television and go out with my mates!' Remember all the times when your teachers and parents said to you, 'You really should join something instead of sitting around every evening'? They weren't wrong...

Still, let's see what we can make of your leisure activities that will look interesting to the shortlister.

Here are some common examples first:

'Watching television and going out with my friends'.

What does it say about you? Answer these questions:

What type of television programmes do you like? Sport? National history? Thrillers? Films? Soaps? Game shows?

What do you do when you go out with your friends? Drink? Go to the cinema? Go clubbing? Attend sporting events? Play sports? Go to concerts?

Do any of your answers to the above relate in any way to the job or course you are interested in? If so, how?

Once you've thought through these questions your answer might now read:

'I enjoy watching television, especially detective stories and sport. I also enjoy seeing films. I socialise regularly with friends, often attending concerts or going bowling.'

This tells the shortlister that you follow some solitary pursuits (watching television), have several different interests (sports, detective stories, music) and you enjoy being with other people.

Here is another example:

'For the past six months I've been hitching around Europe with friends.'

This tells the prospective interviewer that you have initiative and drive, can find your way around, are independent, are flexible (unless you had the whole trip planning in rigid detail before leaving) and can budget (unless of course you frequently wrote home for more funds!).

Get the idea? Looked at this way, what may have seemed a good laugh and of no significance to your future career or education actually tells people quite a lot about you.

So, you could re-word this statement as:

'I enjoy travelling and recently spend six months working my way through Europe with three friends. I particularly enjoy meeting people from other cultures and the sense of challenge and change from day to day.'

Notice that these examples start with the word 'I'. The leisure interests section is an opportunity for you to sell yourself as a real person rather than a list of skills and qualifications. This is more effectively done by writing your interests as part of a personalised sentence rather than simply listing 'reading, swimming, socialising, etc.'.

Here are some other examples:

'I enjoy reading crime novels and watching science fictions films. I also like socialising with friends, often going to classical concerts or to cricket matches.'

'I am keen sportswoman and belong to the school badminton team. I also play tennis and squash. I enjoy reading biographies and watching comedy films.'

'I enjoy model-making and belong to the local Model Making Society. I like playing snooker and spending time with friends.'

'I very much like writing and belong to our local writers' group. I also enjoy reading, particularly political novels and crime stories.'

When you think about completing this section, ask yourself what the person reading it will be looking for. Some possible answers are:

■ a sense that you are a 'rounded' person. This means that you have both solitary and social activities and a reasonably wide range of interests. This, it is hoped, indicates that you are able to work alone and/or with others.

■ something to talk to you about in the interview. This is especially important for university and college interviews when many applicants are saying similar things on their forms. The fact that you did something unusual will give the lecturer something to talk to you about.

■ that your leisure interests in some way reflect the course or job you are applying for. This may be with a particular skill (for example, a practical hobby when applying for a practical job). Some employers actually say that this is the only thing they look for under this section. As you will not know in advance which approach to take you should put any directly relevant interests first in your list. If you put the others first the reader might have stopped reading before they get to the good bits. Alternatively, it may be that the employer is looking for a personality trait that would be useful in the job (playing football may show that you work well as part of a team).

Leisure interests – a word of caution

If you have interests which are likely to ring warning bells with an employer, don't mention them. Such interests might include active membership of a political party, belonging to pressure groups and a lot of involvement in dangerous sports (you might be off sick a lot with broken bones!).

Activity

Now that you've read this section, make a list in your notebook of all your leisure interests and spend some time working out the best way to present this information. Remember, your overall aim is to get an interview for that course or job.

By the way, don't worry if the leisure interest which springs to mind is not something you do regularly. As long as you have done/do it often enough to be able to talk about it sensibly at the interview, you should be okay.

Winning ways with words

By now, you should have a fair idea of the type of information you should present on paper, although there are more tips in later chapters. But for now, let's look at how to show this material effectively.

You've already had some help here (look back to the beginning of this chapter where there were lists of words for ideas of different skills and qualities). Thinking of your qualities and skills, work through these lists until you are happy that you have expressed yourself as accurately as possible.

Now look at the way you've wrapped up those words. Is the overall picture positive and lively or a bit bland? Look at these two examples:

'Reading, going to the cinema, socialising.'

Do you feel you know much about this person? Do they even enjoy these activities? Does her/his personality spring from the page? Compare it with:

'I enjoy reading, particularly thrillers and science fiction. I also like socialising with friends, going to the cinema and concerts.'

Still fairly brief, but much more of a flavour of the person. So, use some 'I' language from time to time, show that *you* are there behind the facts.

It can be quite difficult sometimes to think of positive words and you can end up repeating 'enjoy' several times. Here are some alternatives:

- enthusiastic about
- enthusiasm for
- passion for
- interest in
- fascination for
- attracted to
- curious about
- like
- committed to
- sympathetic to

- pleased with/about
- keen on
- eager to
- excited about
- stimulated by
- delighted with/to/by
- happy about
- exhilarated by/about
- vision for
- skilled in

Likewise, you can present your words positively by using the present tense. Simply the difference between:

'served customers and stocked shelves' and

'serve customers and stock shelves'

A small point, but somehow the present tense sounds more dynamic and appealing.

Activity

Now that you have your list of interests and have considered how to make them sound really positive, write them into one or two sentences. Practise until you are confident they will appeal to a shortlister. Remember though that you may have to re-work this section to fit the requirements of different jobs.

Chapter checklist

This chapter has been about analysing what you have to offer a potential employer. Do you now know:

- the skills you have to offer

- what positive achievements you can discuss

- what makes you stand out from the crowd

- how your referees would describe you

- how you would describe yourself

- what you would say are your strengths

- what your weaknesses are and how you will overcome them

- how you can sell your interests to best effect?

Chapter four
Evidence of success

You should read this chapter:

■ when you begin to think about what to write on your application form or CV.

By the end of this chapter you should know:

■ how to 'sell' your achievements effectively

■ how to present information about awards you have received

■ how and where to show any 'extra special' information about yourself.

Presenting achievements effectively

Having identified your skills by working through Chapter three, you can now begin to define them in a way that should impress any prospective interviewer. Do keep in mind that ultimately everyone is in business to supply a service, whether that is a banking service or a teaching service or anything else. Also, everyone is in the business of survival. An organisation will not survive if it does not make profits. A college will not survive if it has bad lecturers, takes mediocre students and develops a poor reputation.

Therefore it stands to reason that all shortlisters are looking for candidates who are not only going to be successful themselves, but will be successful for the organisation taking them on. Professionalism is the name of the game whether you're applying for a Saturday job or a postgraduate place at university.

All this means that prospective interviewers will be on the look out for people who have that something extra. And very effective 'extras' are those special attributes that bring some degree of fame and glory and which are *measurable*.

> *'I can't believe how many sloppy application forms I receive with no evidence of success in any form at all. Surely applicants must realise that it's a competitive world out there and we can afford to be really choosy who we interview.'*

Quote from a personnel manager

If you are at the very early stages of your career employers will not expect these 'extras' to be world shattering. Some examples of modest but still significant selling points can be found later in this chapter.

How do you show these extras? Well, you need to ask yourself in relation to each skill:

'What evidence can I provide to prove my success in this area?' You do this by thinking in terms of measurable skills, abilities and achievements. For example, how many words can you type a minute, software packages can you use, people you can serve in a day, or items you can sort in an hour.

Also, how much money did you save or earn for the organisation, or time did you save by making that time-saving suggestion? You may even have something to write about what percentage of total sales you made, how quickly you delivered the newspapers, the number of 'thank you' letters you received, how quickly you learned the systems, etc.

Here's a true story about someone who was in a minor position but who achieved something very memorable. John, a mailroom assistant, processed huge volumes of publicity material for his company every week. He pointed out that if each mail-out were one gram lighter they could be posted more cheaply. The literature was altered and the company saved £500,000 per year!

You may not have had John's opportunities, but you may well be able to write something like:

'I built the scenery for the last two school plays.'

'My fund-raising efforts for the charity reached £2,000.'

'I re-organised the layout of the college magazine and sales increased by 5%.'

'I re-organised the way the goods were processed through the stores department and this saved the company £3,000 a year.'

'The experiment I undertook in chemistry highers was later written up for the school magazine.'

'In two years I didn't miss a single day working at my Saturday job.'

'I was the supermarket champion for spotting people trying to pass stolen credit cards.'

If you are applying for a university place then this sort of information becomes part of your 'Personal statement'. The same would be true for an application form. For a CV, you can add this as the 'something special' in relation to a particular job or course, writing at the bottom of your bullet-pointed list. Chapter seven *Dazzling CVs* gives more detail on how to present this.

Activity

Make a note of any extras you can include on your application form or CV. Try to present the information in a *measurable* format. The information below will give you ideas

---

Special responsibilities

Have you held any special responsibilities at school, college, work or in your social life? These might include:

- being a prefect
- chairing meetings
- working on a committee
- being on working parties

- teaching others

- helping at events

- being a monitor

- looking after others

- producing a play

- organising a special event

- escorting guests around the school/college.

Again, many of these items suggest that you have that something extra, over and above the run of the mill person. Additionally, many of them suggest skills that may well be *transferable* to the job or course you seek.

Commendations, prizes and awards

Employers love achievers. If you've been an achiever in the past it shows you're motivated and will probably achieve in the future. Examples of this type of achievement would be Queen's guide or scout, Duke of Edinburgh Award, Head Girl or Boy, or receiving an award for the best dissertation.

Do mention them even if they are not directly relevant, because they say something about the sort of person you are. They suggest that you are:

- more motivated than most people, or

- more hardworking than most people, or

- more academic than most, or

- more conscientious than most people

and that can't be a bad thing.

Publications

If you have ever had anything printed that you have written, mention it. People are always impressed. It doesn't have to be published in a magazine or newspaper. Maybe you had an article in the school or college magazine. Maybe you wrote guidelines on a particular procedure in the workplace. Maybe you wrote an information leaflet.

Where you write this information on your application form or CV will depend rather on how relevant it is to the course or job you are applying for. Looking at university applications first, if the published material is very pertinent to the course, weave a mention of it into the body of your text. If not, you might add it as a final brief sentence at the end of your text.

The same rule generally applies to application forms. If there is nowhere to write it but it's important to mention, do so in the covering letter.

For CVs the situation is different. Make a new heading, 'Articles published' or 'Publications' and list each there. You should give the following information across one line of text for each article.

1.   Name of article/book/publication

2.   Where published

3.   When published

For example:

'Training Methods' *Training Monthly* December 2004

Add a very brief explanation of the context of the publication if it is not clear from the title, e.g.:

'Training Methods' – an overview of the variety of methods available to the trainer when designing a course.

Activity

Make a note of any special achievement and responsibilities, awards or publications you want to mention on an application form or CV. Use the words overleaf.

Positive words to show experience and/or achievement

accomplished	achieved	administered	adapted	assessed
advanced	analysed	applied	benefited	built
controlled	challenged	co-ordinated	conceived	completed
combined	conducted	communicated	compiled	designed
converted	created	delivered	demonstrated	enhanced
developed	devised	diagnosed	directed	economical
effective	efficient	eliminated	enabled	encouraged
exceeded	excelled	established	expanded	experienced
extended	formulated	fulfilled	gained	evolved
guided	identified	implemented	improved	generated
increased	influenced	initiated	innovative	incorporated
instigated	integrated	introduced	launched	led
managed	mounted	minimised	monitored	motivated
organised	persuaded	prepared	participated	perfected
produced	proficient	profitable	progressed	promoted
proposed	performed	quantified	raised	recovered
qualified	redesigned	reorganised	repaired	resolved
resourceful	restored	supervised	revitalised	secured
simplified	sold	solved	specialised	successful
stimulated	terminated	strengthened	trained	transformed

Chapter checklist

- Can you identify those successes you have had in your school or academic career in which an employer or college would be interested?

- Can you identify those successes you have had in your working life that would be interesting to an employer?

- Are you exceptionally good at one particular skill?

- Do you have more knowledge than other people about a particular area?

- Have you noted any special responsibilities you have undertaken?

- Have you received any awards or commendations?

- Have you ever had anything published?

- When you have identified your evidence of success, can you work out the most effective way to present it on your application form, CV or covering letter?

Chapter five
Overcoming common problems

You should read this chapter:

- prior to completing application forms or CVs if you feel you have any 'difficult' information to provide.

By the end of this chapter you should know:

- how to present a variety of potentially difficult information in a way that is positive, or at least limits the damage

- how to minimise your lack of exact fit with the job or course requirements.

Golden rules

It is fairly rare for anyone to be able to look at an advertisement for a job (or a job description) and be able to say, 'This was written for me!' In this chapter we will look at how to get around the lack of ideal fit between what the employer wants and what you've got. But first of all, two golden rules.

The first one is, *if you really like the look of a job, go for it* even if it appears that you are less than ideal. This is particularly true when unemployment is low. What have you got to lose? Even if you waste time completing an application form or CV just to be rejected you can use the work you put in for the next application. One thing you soon learn is that completing application forms can quickly become a chore. So working on one is never wasted because you can copy or adapt what you've written for the next form you complete.

The second rule is *minimise your problem*. Give the information you must provide but don't emphasise the gaps.

For example, what's the point in actually saying (perhaps in your covering letter) 'I know I don't have the .... you require, but am very interested in this job.' Let the reader find out by looking at your form. Never point out the undesirable.

Too young

It's sadly true that we live in an ageist society. You will undoubtedly find that some advertisements state that they are looking for people older than you, although in 2006 there will be legislation against this type of ageism. Well, think positive. Being too young is something that time will cure easily.

I hate to depress you at this stage in your life, but when you reach 40+ you find that people won't want you because you're too old. Time won't cure that one ....

If you are too young for an advertised job (or occasionally a course) apply anyway – remember golden rule number one. It is possible to write a CV (see Chapter nine) that omits dates such as dates of birth. However, your education and career experience dates will probably give you away, especially if you have to complete an application form.

So, give the factual (date) information you have to, but don't in any other way draw attention to your age (such as saying in your covering letter 'I appreciate that I am two years younger than your stated age range'). Remember that, if an employer receives dozens, possibly hundreds, of applications, you will be making it easy for them to reject your application unread.

Instead, just as you would do anyway, emphasise what you *do* have to offer rather than your lack of years. Make the most of your previous experience, thinking through the issues around direct and transferable skills really carefully. Do your best, then sit back and hope for the reward of an interview. If all else fails, just wait until the next time a similar job is advertised – your age may have caught up by then.

Too inexperienced

You may have heard of the expression 'Catch 22'. Basically, it means when you are in a no-win situation. Being too inexperienced is often a catch 22 situation. You can't get the experience without the job and you can't get the job without the experience. Stalemate. However, all is not lost.

In Chapter three you were asked to list *all* your skills and personal qualities. This is a time to consider what skills you have which may be transferable. That is, they may not be exactly the same as those requested, but they may show that you have similar abilities and aptitude. Let's look at some examples.

Example I

As part of your last year at school you undertook some community service. You visited an elderly lady round the corner. You did a bit of shopping for her, read to her and generally kept her company. Now you're thinking that you'd like to apply for a job in a day nursery. In many ways the two seem quite different, but a lot of skills are general and transferable. Both require that you get on with people, have patience, have the ability to listen and care, are able to understand the other person's point of view. They also need you to be trustworthy and be a good communicator.

This is a good list and one that would interest any prospective nursery employer.

These are your *transferable skills* and are essential to any job that involves working with people. And think about that. It is not only in the 'caring' professions that you need to work with people. These skills would be equally valuable to a bank clerk, a doctor, a vet, a solicitor, and even a car mechanic. Looked at from the customer's point of view, who would not be happy to deal with anyone in any profession who had these qualities?

Example 2

During the summer vacation at college, you and three friends went hitching and working around Europe. You did a variety of jobs to earn enough money to keep travelling. They included waiting at table, washing up, and grape picking. Now, at the end of your course, you want to apply for a job as a management trainee for a finance house. Apart from your qualifications you can offer:

- money handling experience (okay, on a smaller scale I admit)

- using your initiative

- experience of foreign currencies

- working as part of a team

- being hardworking

- experience in European travel

- knowledge of other cultures

- personal budgeting skills

- crisis handling skills (well, there probably would have been at least one after all).

These transferable skills would be invaluable in any number of other jobs, for example banking, travel agencies, translating, social work, nursing, and teaching.

Get the idea? The jobs you are interested in may not actually specify these qualities, but it is worth looking carefully at the details of the job and thinking through the types of situation someone doing it might face.

Suppose you went to work for a large supermarket chain as a trainee manager. Crisis handling skills would be very valuable if you found yourself confronted with a shoplifter, someone using a stolen credit card, a severe staff shortage or a customer having a heart attack. Just because a job doesn't specify crisis-handling skills, it doesn't mean they don't have crises or won't think this an asset.

Health problems

There are no strict guidelines for disclosing health problems. There are, however, some which are 'traditionally' mentioned on application forms. These are health problems like epilepsy, and physical disabilities which may affect the way a job is done. Some other complaints, such as diabetes or slight hearing or visual problems, are 'invisible' and you should use your judgement about whether to mention them. This judgement could be based on the type of work you are applying for and the extent of your disability. If you have a more serious disability speak to your Jobcentre/Jobcentre Plus for advice.

There is legislation against discrimination (the Disability Discrimination Act) and employers have a duty to employ you if you are the best candidate for the job and they can do so with 'reasonable adaptation' to building or equipment or with you having a helper.

The DDA Helpline provides information and advice about all aspects of the DDA and can advise on specialist organisations to contact if necessary. It also offers practical advice on employment for disabled people. The telephone number is 0800 882200. Textphone service: 0800 243355. Their website is www.disability.gov.uk email: feedback-disability@dwp.gsi.gov.uk

Also, some employers belong to what's called the 'Green Tick' scheme. This means that they guarantee to interview anyone with a disability who meets the essential criteria they have said is necessary for the job.

Wrong qualifications

One of the really tough things about our education system is that we have to make choices about which subjects to take at a time when most of us haven't a clue what we want to do with our lives. This can mean that the choices we made at 14 can affect our chances of achieving the goals we set ourselves at 16 or 18 or 20. Well unfortunately we can't turn back the clock, so we have to work with what we've got.

If you are thinking of applying for a college place in a different subject area, ask yourself *'How can I sell this 'odd' application to the college?'* Let's therefore imagine that you took all science subjects at school but now want to do an arts course. Why? How can you really convince the reader that this is an abiding interest and not just a passing whim? Can your headteacher or whoever writes the letter to your college back up your application with examples?

For some subjects, it would be very unlikely that you could get a place without prior learning and science would be one of these. Can you apply to a college which has an introductory year of some sort in your chosen subject area?

By the way, this is another situation where simply getting older helps. Many colleges are much more relaxed about entry qualifications for older students, believing that they have the self-knowledge and motivation to study hard and see the course through.

If you are applying for a job which specifies different qualifications to your own many of the same points apply. How can you convince the prospective interviewer that, despite the 'wrong' qualifications, you have sufficient knowledge and skill to handle the job? Do you have valuable experience if not the qualifications? Do you have similar, transferable skills? In times of high unemployment there are likely to be many people with the 'right' qualifications applying for a job, but remember 'nothing ventured nothing gained'. You definitely won't get the job if you don't apply for it ... If unemployment is low, employers can't afford to be so choosy and you will stand a much better chance.

Murky past

Do you have any skeletons in your cupboard? Did you for example, get excluded from school for cheating in an exam? skip lot of classes? get in trouble with the law? job hop for the past two years? get sacked from your last job? have a reputation for laziness?

Well, if you can answer 'yes' to any of these types of question, the next question has to be, *'Does anyone have to know?'*. The answer is *It depends* on the sort of college place or job you are applying for.

If you got excluded or truanted a lot, for example, it may be mentioned in any letter or reference from your school to a college or employer and there is little you can do about that. However, if you are genuinely a reformed character and had time to prove it, you could ask the teacher either not to mention earlier problems or to say how your situation and behaviour have improved.

For some jobs trouble with the law won't count, but with others they're vitally important. If you helped your dad with a bullion raid, a bank might think twice about you. Agencies working with children would definitely not look at you if you had a history of abusing children.

You should never lie on an application form or CV. But remember, some questions simply aren't asked at the paper stage and it is up to the interviewer to ask those questions at the interview itself. If you *do* have to write about these issues and they are part of your 'youthful indiscretion' as it is called, you may want to point out that you've grown up a bit since then and are keen to be successful in your chosen course or career. Again, see if you can get someone who will give you a reference which will confirm this. Many employers understand that teenagers occasionally do daft things and, as long as they think the worm has turned, they will often overlook minor problems.

> *One applicant wrote, 'As a Christian, I enjoy helping other people, and as a Christian I believe that I would have a lot to offer your sort of work.' Altogether this person mentioned being a Christian six times on the application form. There's nothing wrong with being a Christian of course, but this person came across as if she could think of nothing else. We are a charity, but not a religious one and it seemed inappropriate to give this one aspect of her life such emphasis.'*

> **Quote from the manager of a charitable organisation**

Lack of leisure interests

Chapter three provides you with ideas on how to overcome any lack of 'desirable' leisure interests.

However, you should be wary of writing anything that might trigger prejudice in the reader. If this is the case, the 'leisure interests' section is where it is most likely to show. If you're an active member of a political party, for example, the reader's politics might not match your own.

Overcoming prejudice

One of the strange things about human beings is that we want two different things which are difficult to achieve at the same time. We want to be treated as an individual to give us a sense of identity, and yet we also want to be treated as part of a group to give us a sense of belonging.

Sadly, for many people, being part of a group (their 'in group') is only significant if there is an 'out group' to be against. Take football supporters for example or those supporting either Oxford or Cambridge teams in the boat race. For many people, to be *for* one thing means you must be *against* another.

This means that unfortunately, many people are walking bundles of prejudice, it's just that different people are prejudiced against different things. We could, for example, be prejudiced against people with blue eyes or those with a second toe longer than their big toe. Luckily, most people have only mild prejudices and do not act on them.

However, there are some fairly common prejudices and these are usually based around easily observable *differences*. People are often fearful of others they see as in some way different. These differences include ethnic origin, gender, religion, sexuality, age, disability, politics, class, accent or lifestyle.

In Great Britain there is currently legislation against discrimination on the grounds of gender, race, disability, religion or sexuality (legislation against ageism is due in 2006). This means that these are the only areas where you will have legal backing if you can prove discrimination. And proving such discrimination is a problem in itself.

The difficulty is that unless you know the person opening your envelope you don't know if you are dealing with a prejudiced person or not. I prefer to be optimistic and trust that people are fair. However, this is not always the case. There has been quite a lot of publicity about Asian law students who have tried to get work with law firms. Even the top students who have exceptionally high grades fail to get interviews. One such person, an Asian woman, was second in her year at college – a brilliant student. She applied for literally dozens of jobs and failed to even get an interview for most of them. A London borough eventually employed her in their legal department. She later became head of the Equal Opportunities Commission!

Likewise, in some circles there is still prejudice against women (and occasionally against men). There's still a long way to go before everyone is treated equally.

All of which leaves you with the need to make a decision about how to handle prejudice. Do you have a foreign sounding name? Are you are female applying for work in a traditionally male job market, or vice versa? How can you handle this? You could consider not mentioning your religion or political beliefs in the 'Additional information' section, or you could use only initials instead of your first name on your application form or CV. In fact, many equal opportunities employers only ask for this. And if it is relevant you could avoid including interests that indicate your sexuality or lifestyle if these might be considered 'alternative'.

Of course, you shouldn't have to do any of these things, but you may decide to play safe.

If you are absolutely sure that you are being discriminated against, you can take your case up with either:

Commission for Racial Equality

St Dunstan's House, 201-211 Borough High Street, London SE1 1GZ. Tel 020 7939 0000. Fax 020 7939 0001. Email info@cre.gov.uk or one of their local offices. You can find their details on their website www.cre.gov.uk

or for gender issues for Great Britain:

Equal Opportunities Commission

Arndale House, Arndale Centre, Manchester M4 3EQ. Tel: 0845 601 5901. Fax: 0161 838 1733. Email info@eoc.org.uk www.eoc.org.uk/

or for Scotland:

St Stephens House, 279 Bath Street, Glasgow G2 4JL. Tel: 0845 601 5901. Fax: 0141 248 5834. Email: scotland@eoc.org.uk

or for Wales:

Windsor House, Windsor Lane, Cardiff CF10 3GE. Tel: 029 2064 1079. Fax: 029 2064 1079.

or for London:

36 Broadway, London SW1H 0BH. Tel: 020 7222 1110. Fax: 020 7222 2810. Email: media@eoc.org.uk

or for disability:

DRC Helpline

FREEPOST, MIDO 2064, Stratford upon Avon CV37 9BR. Tel: 08457 622 633. Textphone: 08457 622 644. Fax: 08457 778 878. www.drc-gb.org/whatwedo/helplineservices.asp

Disabled applicants can also get help from Jobcentre Plus, their website is www.jobcentreplus.gov.uk.

There is also legislation against discrimination on the grounds of sexuality and religion. You can easily find more details on the internet.

Chapter checklist

■ If you are really too young for the job you want, go for it anyway and let the employer know what a lot you have to offer.

■ If you don't have sufficient experience, sell what experience you have and remember transferable skills from other areas of your ability.

- If you have health problems, consider whether to disclose them or not. Some are always disclosed, others are discretionary. Get advice from your Jobcentre/Jobcentre Plus or the Disability Rights Commission.

- If you don't have the right qualifications and are keen on the job, apply anyway. They may not get anyone with the right qualifications and even if they do you may have other attributes that they consider more important.

- If you have some skeletons in your cupboard, think about how to present them in the best light. See if you can find someone who will give you a reference stating that you are a reformed character (assuming you are!)

- Think carefully about your leisure interests and how to present them. If you genuinely don't have any, get off the sofa or away from the screen and find some…

- Be careful about disclosing information that could arouse the shortlister's prejudice – comments about politics or religion, for example.

Chapter six
University and college applications

You should read this chapter:

- when you are thinking about completing your UCAS or college of further education application form.

By the end of this chapter you should know:

- how to complete the factual section of your form

- how to present yourself positively in the 'Personal Statement' section.

UCAS application forms

Applicants for undergraduate places on courses in universities and colleges of higher education have to complete a UCAS application form irrespective of which college they are applying for. Full-time programmes of study leading to an academic award, HNC, HND, DipHE or first degree qualifications should be made through UCAS.

> *'Schools are very good about giving a lot of help to students to complete the form in the best possible way. Despite that, some still come through which are dreary to read and fill me with no enthusiasm to meet the person.'*

Quote from a college lecturer

There are two ways to apply. Electronically – using the 'apply' system or the electronic application system (EAS) – or the traditional way through a paper application form.

UCAS forms on the web

At the appropriate time of year UCAS has details of their application form on the web: www.ucas.com/getting/apply05 at the time of writing. If your school, college or Connexions/careers centre has signed up to use the '**Apply**' system, you can apply direct to UCAS online.

Other schools will be using the **EAS system** (Electronic Application System). This allows you to complete your form at home on your PC, or use that of your college or Connexions/careers centre. To apply in this way you must go through a school, college, Connexions/careers service. However, EAS is being phased out – 2005 entry will be the last year of EAS.

Paper applications – you can also apply using the UCAS paper-based system, although this will also be phased out over the next few years.

Also on the UCAS website is advice on how to complete the form. You can obtain the form through your school or college, or direct from UCAS, at UCAS Enquiries, UCAS, PO Box 28, Cheltenham GL52 3LZ. Tel: 0870 1122211 Monday-Friday 08.30-17.00. Email: enquiries@ucas.ac.uk for an automated response providing general information and guidance on UCAS procedures.

There is excellent advice on how to complete the factual section of the UCAS form in the booklet which you will receive with the form and for that reason no further advice is given on this here. DO READ THROUGH THIS INFORMATION CAREFULLY BEFORE YOU BEGIN – it will save you time, effort and frustration.

Here we will concentrate on Section 10 – Personal Statement. This is the section where you come alive as a person as opposed to a collection of facts.

Here is what a lecturer in a teacher training college had to say about some of the application forms she has seen:

The applications from prospective student teachers include an application form, a covering letter and a letter of application.

When I read through the forms prior to interview I look for a real commitment to wanting to teach. Candidates must show that they have done some work with youngsters. I don't want to think that they have just decided 'oh, it might be a good idea to work with children'. I need to see a real commitment to the work.

I like to be convinced, even on paper, that there is a sense of real warmth towards children. That can come across even on the application form because of the way they describe the work they have done with children in the past.

Sadly, some prospective students come across as very naive and not very politically (with a small p) aware. That is, they don't seem to know what's going on in the teaching world, they don't seem to have read the Times Educational Supplement, nor to be aware of current issues in education. We would like to see this type of awareness on the application form because we want to know that students are aware that the job is a difficult one and that finding employment at the end of the course is not easy.

When I read through the forms they are sometimes so poor that I suspect that they don't show them to anyone else before they send them off. I suppose it could feel a bit embarrassing for some people to do so, but it would be of real help to get an objective view before they put the form in the post. After all, they must know that people are going to read them at the college. If they did get someone else to check them, they wouldn't make such basic mistakes. They really need to find someone they can trust to go through their application form with them and to question them on it.

For example, during the interview I will often take a phrase out of a person's letter of application and start my question by saying, 'you say in your letter of application....' This means that if they haven't thought through a statement they've made they can be left with egg on their face at interview. When completing an application form, students should always have the interview in mind as well.

Sometimes after I've actually interviewed the person I feel a need to go back to re-read their application form to see if what they wrote ties up with what they were saying.

With regard to references, sometimes I am horrified at the wording in references. One head of department had written, 'This student is not academically bright but will make an excellent primary school teacher'.

One big question I always keep in mind – 'would I want this person to teach my child for a year?'

Section 10: Personal statement

That blank page can be easy! First a few practical tips. Make a copy of the form before you start and practise on that. Then, when you are happy with what you've written, remember to write, photocopy or print into the space in the page itself. Do not attach the information on a piece of paper or stick paper over it. To wordprocess the page follow these instructions:

1. In Word go to File, then Page Setup and set margins to top 8.2cm, bottom 4.5cm, left 1cm and right 1cm (or bigger numbers than these but not smaller).

2. Then go to Format, Paragraph, and set After to 6pt (then your name and paragraphs will be spaced properly)

3. Use font size 12 or bigger as this is a UCAS requirement.

4. Type your name on the first line in the centre.

5. If you are not completing your form in one go, remember to save it so that you can return and complete it.

6. Before you print it onto the UCAS form, print it onto plain paper or better still a photocopy of the relevant page, and check that it will fit.

7. When you print onto the form, do it before you complete the rest of the form in case of any mishaps – it'll save you a lot of re-writing.

8. Remember, you must NOT stick paper onto this page.

The instructions on how to complete the application form provided by UCAS provide you with some excellent headings on what to put in this section. These headings are:

- Why you have chosen the courses you have listed.

- What interests you about your chosen subject. (Include details of what you have read about the subject.)

- Career plans.

- Any job, work experience, placement or voluntary work you have done, particularly if it is relevant to your subject.

- Details of non-accredited skills and achievements you have gained through activities such as Young Enterprise, Duke of Edinburgh Award, or the ASDAN Youth Award Scheme.

- Other achievements, such as The Liverpool Curriculum Enrichment Programme (CEP), or Diploma of Achievement.

- Your future plans.

- Any subjects you are studying that do not have a formal assessment.

- Any sponsorship or placements you have or have applied for.

- If you are planning to take a year out, your reasons why.

- Your social, sports or leisure interests.

You may want to include information from your national record of achievement or Progress File, if you have one.

For international students, the following questions should also be answered:

- Why do you want to study in the UK?

- What evidence do you have to show that you can complete a higher education course that is taught in English? Please say if some of your studies have been assessed in English.

- Have you had a position of authority or used your communication skills in any activity?

I strongly recommend that you read Chapter ten, *Job application forms* (particularly the section headed 'The dreaded blank page'), before you start this section because much of the advice there is relevant.

Many people really hate completing this section but think of this as a piece of work; an essay on the world's most interesting person – you. Suddenly it seems much more appealing. What do you do with any essay?

You:

■ read the question and attempt to fully understand what is expected of you

■ read all the relevant material to formulate an answer

■ select those aspects of the material needed for your essay, rejecting those which are inappropriate

■ plan how to present your information, considering all aspects, angles and arguments

■ write an essay plan

■ do a draft

■ refine it as many times as it takes to get it right

■ make a good copy.

And that's exactly what you have to do with this section. Don't even expect to polish it off in one sitting. Start the work and then leave it for a few hours or a day, mulling it over in your mind as you go about the rest of your life. Once you have decided on what to say, polish and polish it until it gleams. It should take you several goes. Remember to get one or two other people to read it before you send it off, preferably a teacher.

The chapters on CV writing give you a list of positive words you can use you describe yourself and your achievements; you might want to refer back to them when you get started.

Remember, your work in completing this form is for two purposes. First, to get you an interview and secondly to give you something to talk about at the interview.

Hopefully, one will follow on smoothly from the other. If you have been working through this book you will already have in your notebook details of your skills, experience, education, character, interests, leisure activities, strengths and weaknesses and special awards, etc. But don't include any weaknesses on this form!

You have also considered how to overcome common problems you might face. If you haven't, read through the chapter on Dazzling CVs and follow the advice there now.

Remebering what the teacher training college lecturer had to say at the beginning of this section, do keep in mind current issues in the area of your choice. You can get information on this from your school, professional or trade journals (your central library will probably have them), talking to people already doing the job your course could lead to. You could also research by looking in newspapers and the media generally, the internet or speaking to existing students.

This is where you put together all this work in a sparkling and riveting way ...

Activity

Here is an example of what someone might write for Section 10. Work through the paragraphs asking yourself what you like and would change about it. (I've numbered each paragraph for reference later):

1. *I am applying for the business studies HND course because I am interested in business and I want a good career.*

2. *I have become interested in business because my father works in a bank and I realise that I must get a good qualification to start my career in a junior management position.*

3. *I worked in a building society for three weeks for work experience. I know that this isn't quite the same as a bank but I learnt a lot of useful things.*

4. *I am currently taking seven GCSEs including business studies which I enjoy very much. I particularly like learning about the way the financial world works.*

5. *My ambition is to be a bank manager or to work for a large finance company.*

6. *I enjoy playing netball, and going to the cinema. I also enjoy embroidery and am a keen photographer.*

> 7. *I have just passed my First Aid Certificate with the British Red Cross.*
>
> 8. *I have not yet secured an industrial placement, but have applied to three banks and am awaiting their response.*
>
> 9. *I do not wish to defer my application to next year.*
>
> Do not read any further until you have completed this exercise.

General points

The first think to note is that nearly every paragraph started with 'I' (not uncommonly seen on such forms). Try to make your beginnings more varied.

Further, the whole thing is a bit disjointed with no 'flow' to the content. Although it provides quite a lot of relevant information, it is stilted and uninspiring. Many of the points should be expanded further.

Remember, there are eleven areas you are asked to cover in this section. Do check that you have covered each one and present your information in the order shown on page 3 of the application form. It makes it easier for the reader to 'shortlist' you for interview.

Specific points

As mentioned above, this example does not answer all points in order as you should. Do please do so when you complete your form.

Here are some suggestions as to how each paragraph could be improved. You may have thought of others.

1. *I am applying for the Business Studies HND course because I am interested in business and I want a good career.*

This is clearly far too brief an answer. The student should have mentioned:

- why s/he wanted this particular course as opposed to one run by any other college. This would include mentioning specific aspects of the course which may differ from those offered elsewhere. It may be relevant to discuss the type of college, or teaching or college location if these have a particular bearing on the application.

- information about being interested in business and career aspirations should preferably be all in one place. In this example they are dotted around rather disjointedly.

2. *I have become interested in business because my father works in a bank and I realise that I must get a good qualification to start my career in a junior management position.*

It can be helpful to show that there is a family tradition of working in a particular field because it shows that you are likely to have a deeper than average knowledge of the work and that you are likely to get support from your family. It also means that you are likely to have realistic expectations about career structures.

However, the two halves of the sentence don't really 'hang together'. There are better ways to word the whole lot, but at the very least there should be a full stop after the word 'bank'. Perhaps the first half could read, 'I feel that I have a good understanding of business from a banking perspective as my father works in a bank. This means that I am very familiar with the type of work involved.' (it may even be helpful here to give examples, and in a completely re-written version these examples could be linked to the work experience in a building society).

The second half of the sentence would probably be better elsewhere – perhaps as part of the 'reasons for applying for this course' section.

3. *I worked in a building society for three weeks for work shadowing. I know that this isn't quite the same as a bank but I learnt a lot of useful things.*

Ouch! What a lot of missed opportunities here. For a start, never put yourself or your skills down ('I know it isn't quite the same' – the reader knows that too, there's no need to emphasise it). Here are some pointers about this section:

- It doesn't give any feeling of enthusiasm. The person is saying they want to work in this type of environment, but gives no indication of having enjoyed it.

- There is much overlap between working in a building society and working in a bank, especially as building societies offer many banking facilities. This means that this person would have learned many transferable skills which could have been mentioned. These would include dealing with people, handling money, filing, understanding systems, answering the telephone, liaising with other branches and using a computer. You may think of other things.

- This section could also have mentioned the aspects of the work which the applicant particularly enjoyed and those s/he is keen to learn more about (ensuring of course that the course being applied for covers these points ...). This would have demonstrated that the applicant was familiar with the course content and provided something to talk about at interview.

4. *I am currently taking seven GCSEs including business studies which I enjoy very much. I particularly like learning about the way the financial world works.*

This is better inasmuch as it shows some enthusiasm. However the applicant could have enlarged further on the aspect of the business studies course which s/he enjoyed. It would also be worth noting any other related topics to business studies – an obvious example would be maths if the person is thinking about going into banking. Another example would be any course which involved analytical thinking as business studies would certainly require this. Again, this would be a transferable skill. Another useful thing to do would be to highlight how any aspects of any of her/his studies had proved valuable on work experience.

5. *My ambition is to be a bank manager or to work for a large finance company.*

Well, I know this a separate topic as suggested in the *Information for applicants*, but do remember that those headings are simply suggestions. This one liner does nothing to enhance the quality of the application and simply repeats information provided elsewhere.

6. *I enjoy playing netball, and going to the cinema. I also enjoy embroidery and am a keen photographer.*

This is a good start, and the fact that the applicant has time to pursue leisure interests as well as study will be seen positively by the reader. Also, it shows that the applicant has some social and some solitary interests which are quite varied – remember that this shows a 'rounded person'.

However, it could be much improved:

- The word 'enjoy' is used twice in two sentences. Use instead another similar word.

- It might interest the reader to know who the applicant plays netball for. The school? A local team? A national team? Does the applicant have any special responsibilities as part of the team, perhaps organising return matches or refreshments.

- Netball is a team game. A business studies course is sure to involve some team working, probably working on a business project with other students. It would therefore be worth mentioning that you enjoy being part of a team.

- Although it is unlikely that the cinema going will link directly with the college course, if the applicant enjoys one particular type of film it could just be mentioned ('especially thrillers'). This is unlikely to help in getting an interview but might give the interviewer something to talk about if they enjoy the same films (never hurts to have something in common with the interviewer).

- Embroidery shows attention to detail, a skill needed in business. A connection could be made here.

- What sort of photography? General? Still life? Birds? People? Sunsets? Like the cinema visits, it may pay to enlarge just a little on this section.

7. *I have just passed my First Aid Certificate with the British Red Cross.*

Although this is a non-examined subject it could also have gone under 'Interests', although no harm is done where it is. If I read this though I would wonder why this person chose to do this course. It may be that there is a reason, such as helping in a Brownie pack which s/he has omitted to mention (you need a lot of leadership skills to run any sort of group).

8. *I have not yet secured an industrial placement, but have applied to three banks and am awaiting their response.*

This is fine although perhaps a little more detail would help. Which banks? Is the applicant hopeful of the outcome?

9. *I do not wish to defer my application to next year.*

It is worth stating whether or not you plan to defer your entry and take year out. If you are going to, say what your plans are for the year out.

There you have it, one 'Personal Statement' section analysed. Now it's your turn:

> *'What students have to remember is that we read literally dozens of application forms each year. I certainly love to see one that stands out from the crowd in some way. I think 'Oh good, this'll be an interesting interview'.'*

Quote from a college lecturer

Sample completed Section 10

I am applying for the degree in social work because this is a career I feel very enthusiastic about.

At present I am studying A levels in psychology, English and sociology and taking one additional GCSE in human biology. I am particularly enjoying psychology because of the understanding it has given me into why people behave as they do. Whilst psychology provides this knowledge from an individual perspective, sociology looks at what makes people tick from the other end of the spectrum – society. Additionally I have studied a Diploma of Achievement course on probability and risk as I believe that much social work involves assessing risk.

In year 9, I undertook a two-week work placement in a residential home for elderly people and very much enjoyed working with both staff and residents. I came into contact regularly with other people in various caring professions and have a good grasp of the concept of partnership working. This, plus conversations with my mother (a social worker) and her colleagues, has given me a good insight into the issues faced by social workers.

> *I am a pupil mentor for our school and am currently mentoring two year 7 students. Our training for this role was very relevant and covered understanding people, and listening and questioning skills.*
>
> *I do not plan to take a year out.*
>
> *My interests are socialising with friends, being a member of an amateur dramatics group and reading 'family' novels. I have learned the value of team work through the dramatics group and can also use my initiative readily.*

Chapter checklist

Have you:

- got the right form? Applicants to universities and colleges of higher education have to complete a UCAS form, applicants for colleges of further education mostly complete a UCAS form also although a few still have their own form. This will be different for each college

- photocopied the form at least once before you start? Work on the copy so that you don't have to worry about mistakes

- followed the instructions exactly

- presented factual information in a consistent and clear way

- regarded the 'Personal Statement' section as a piece of work in its own right? It will need careful preparation and planning

- remembered that the reader may also be the interviewer? They read many forms and will be pleased to read something well written and interesting

- shown that you are really interested in the subject you are applying for

- mentioned any work or research you have done in your subject area?

Chapter seven
Dazzling CVs

You should read this chapter:

- when you need to prepare a CV for either a specific job or for a general mailing to a number of organisations.

By the end of this chapter you should know:

- what a CV is

- the advantages and disadvantages of this method of presenting information about yourself

- how to use advertisements, job descriptions and person specifications to help you to construct your CV

- about CV templates on your PC and electronic CVs.

What is a CV?

The term CV is an abbreviation for Curriculum Vitae, which means 'the course of your life' although employers will only be interested in your life as it relates to the job they have to offer.

The good (and perhaps bad) news about writing a CV (called a resume in some countries) is that there is no single 'correct' way of writing one.

To get you thinking about the issues around writing a CV here is what a partner of an independent residential resource for young people in need had to say on the subject. He had recently been interviewing for residential workers.

'From a basic point of view I'm looking for writing skills because people have to keep records, etc. I'm also looking for people who have a fair amount of life experience, not necessarily in terms of years, but what they've fitted into those years. I'm looking to see whether they can use very little space to show that they have a good grasp of what the job is, how well thought out their application is and what they can offer the job — rather than that they've just seen the job and salary and thought 'I'll have a go at that'. In terms of the job description and person specification, I'm checking to see if the essential requirements are met. If the desirable qualities are met too, that's a real bonus. I try to use the essential and desirable qualities as a way of being very objective and shortlisting on an equal opportunities basis.

One of the young women in our project was looking for a hairdressing job. She sent off a letter to a lot of local employers which included a lot of CV material. As a result of that she got offered quite a lot of interviews. One of the shops gave her a job. These were people who weren't actually advertising at the time — she got the names from the Yellow Pages.

We'd helped her to word her CV / letter in such a way that it helped to show her personality and allowed the prospective employer to anticipate the sort of person who would be sitting in front of them if they offer her an interview.

If unemployment is high, your CV has to stand out in some way. And your personality is one way in which you can stand above the others and stop your details from going in the bin with the others.

The message to applicants has to be that interviewers who are looking to appoint someone ask themselves as they read, 'What's so special about you? Why should I interview you? What sort of motivation and investment do you have in the job?' The fact that people feel good about themselves (which is a positive point) should come across on paper.'

Advantages and disadvantages of the CV

Advantages

Because there is no single right way to present a CV and because so many people do it poorly, it gives you an opportunity to shine over the opposition if you make a good job of yours. Also, unlike when you are completing application forms, when you write a CV it is you who decides what to include. And because you choose the CV headings yourself, you can have a separate heading for any unusual work or academic information you wish to present. This is especially useful if you want to emphasise the point. This can be difficult in the little box application forms usually provide for 'Additional information'. For example, I always have a separate heading for 'Publications'. Again, because you choose the headings yourself, you can miss out any information you prefer not to include. This information might include periods of unemployment or poor examination results.

CV preparation is an excellent way of training your mind to present information succinctly. This may be of real help to you when preparing for an interview. The CV is an excellent 'crib sheet' if you are invited to interview. It will help you to think through what you could be asked about.

Disadvantages

It can feel as if you have to make the whole thing up from scratch each time. Actually when you have done the work once (by working through this chapter), you will only need to revise it rather than re-write it in future because the bulk of the work will be done.

CVs leave little space for the sort of wider discussion of your abilities you can sometimes provide on the blank page on application forms headed 'Information in support of your application' or similar.

You really need to use a typewriter or wordprocessor to produce a well-presented CV. However, it is much more acceptable to complete an application form by hand, especially as many people have wordprocessors only and it is difficult to make information fit the boxes allocated on the form.

CV style

If you are preparing a CV get it wordprocessed. This makes it easier to make alterations or move text around. You can vary the font size and type. You have a thesaurus and spell checker to assist you and can even check your grammar. And, bearing in mind that you should adapt your CV for each job, the best point about wordprocessing is the ease with which you can adapt it.

But don't use too many fonts on the same document or it looks messy (three is generally considered the maximum). Also, don't go crazy with font sizes; be consistent with what you use for what information and don't use a font that is difficult to read.

Most people use one of three fonts:

Comic Sans MS – this is very popular at the moment and looks very up-to-date

Times New Roman – was one of the most popular until recently, still very commonly used

Arial – another popular choice

Don't use too many different ways of emphasising information. Your choice is <u>underlining</u>, or making text **bold**, or making text *italicised*, or altering text size. Remember to be consistent with how you use these ways of emphasising points.

There is more information about CV layout in the next chapter.

CV content

Even more important than the style and layout of your CV is the content. We need to consider *what you're actually going to write*. This takes a bit of time, although of course you don't have to do it all in one go.

Initially, we'll assume you are preparing a CV in response to a particular job advertisement, rather than just sending CVs out 'uninvited' (some tips on dealing with 'on spec' CVs will be covered in the next chapter). To do this you need to gather together before you start:

- the information you noted about yourself

- the job advertisement

- the job description

- the person specification (if one is supplied)

- any other information you have about the organisation

- plenty of scrap paper (or a new file on your wordprocessor).

Let me take you back a step in case you are not clear about some of the terms.

A **job description** describes the job to be done. This usually consists of a list of the main tasks involved in the work. Some employers write alongside each task the percentage of time spent on that task or sometimes indicate how important each task is. Most employers also have a final 'catch-all' heading along the lines of 'And anything else your manager tells you to do'!

A **person specification** describes the person who can do the job. Some organisations call the person specification 'competencies'. This will be a list of personal and professional attributes the employer is looking for in the postholder. It is very common for this list to be split in some way into 'essential' and 'desirable' qualities. When looking through all the application forms or CVs the employer will be looking for people who can at least meet all the 'essential' requirements. If there are several or a lot of these, he or she will then seek out those applicants who also have as many as possible of the 'desirable' qualities.

So, as mentioned in Chapter two, someone looking for a wordprocessing operator might have 'Type all correspondence for three managers' in the job description list (this describes the task to be done, and identifies clearly the skills the person needs to have). In the person specification list it would read something like 'Able to type at 45 wpm'.

Another example would be an employer who doesn't actually need a non-smoker because the workplace is not subject to any particular hygiene regulations, but who seeks a non-smoker to comply with company policy.

You may have applied for the job but not been sent a job description, person specification or any information about the organisation. If so, you need to do some basic detective work. Here is a step-by-step guide:

Phone the organisation and ask if they can provide you with any of these documents. If they can't, and you are unclear exactly what the job will involve, ask if you can speak to the human resources (sometimes called personnel) manager, or whoever is dealing with the vacancy, to get more details. Remember when you do this that you need to sound polished and confident, because the conversation (as well as your CV) might affect your chances of an interview.

If this is still not possible, phone your local Connexions/careers centre or Jobcentre/Jobcentre Plus office to see if they can give you any clues. They may not be able to help with the person specification but will almost certainly be able to give some ideas about what the type of job might involve. They are also likely to know something about most employers in your region, especially if they have used the Jobcentre/Jobcentre Plus service to fill a vacancy.

Look for further information about the organisation. This may be:

■ word of mouth; find out what other people know about them

■ by keeping an eye on the local press

■ by looking in the national press or internet if it's a big organisation

■ by looking in trade or professional journals (your main library will probably have them)

■ looking on the web.

From this basic information you can work out for yourself what the person specification is likely to include. Later in this chapter there are a couple of job descriptions and person specifications that will give you a further idea of the connection between the two.

Working out a person specification from a job description and advertisement

If you aren't provided with a person specification it is very helpful to try to work out for yourself what might be in it. That way you can focus the information you provide more meaningfully. Of course, you can never be exactly sure of what the person specification might say. However, you can make a reasonably intelligent guess and probably pick up most of the main points. Here is one example to show you how to do it. We'll start with the advertisement which will give you some valuable information.

NIGHT SHIFT WORKER

MACHINE OPERATOR

Tasty Bread Products Ltd are seeking three additional night shift workers to help produce our high quality bread products.

Applicants should have good health and have good general education. Full training given although experience of this type of work would be an advantage.

Basic pay £XX for a 41 hour week, four weeks' annual holiday and good working conditions.

For details, contact:
Mrs Singh, Tasty Bread Products Ltd
Broomfield Road, Manchester M12 3RR
Tel: xxxxxxxxx

Now look at the job description:

TASTY BREAD PRODUCTS LTD

JOB DESCRIPTION
MACHINE OPERATOR

Machine operators are accountable to the Production Supervisor, Mr G. Smith. The main tasks of the job are to:

1. ensure that the correct ingredients are added to machines to guarantee production to the correct standards

2. follow the progress of the mixture to the next stage of processing

3. ensure hygiene standards are achieved

4. make adjustments to the machine as necessary to ensure smooth operation

5. report any faults

6. clean the machine at the end of the shift.

Now you've got a wealth of information.

Activity

Read through the advertisement and job description on the previous page carefully and underline any words that you think are important. Do not read any further until this activity is complete.

Here are the points I feel are important:

NIGHT SHIFT WORKER
MACHINE OPERATOR

Tasty Bread Products Ltd are seeking three additional night shift workers to help produce our high quality bread products.

Applicants should have good health and have good general education. Full training given although experience of this type of work would be an advantage.

Basic pay £XX for a 41 hour week, four weeks' annual holiday and good working conditions.

For details, contact:
Mrs Singh, Tasty Bread Products Ltd
Broomfield Road, Manchester M12 3RR
Tel: xxxxxxxxx

Now, what sort of person would they be looking for to undertake this type of work? (This tells you what they would put in a person specification.)

Here are some factors that might well be included in the person specification:

1. The indication of good health suggests they also want someone who is **fit**, or at least **won't take a lot of time off sick**.

2. The emphasis on correct ingredients suggests a need for **attention to detail**.

3. The person must be **observant** in order to ensure that the mixture is progressing satisfactorily (and also to note whether the machine is operating properly).

4. The person must be **clean and tidy** in order to maintain hygiene standards.

5. The person must be **thorough** in order to clean the machine properly (food manufacturers can incur huge fines if their machinery is dirty).

6. The person must be **able to use their own initiative** to decide whether to try to fix a fault him/herself or to report it to someone else.

I am sure that this working environment would also be one where people would not be allowed to smoke.

There you have it. Knowing nothing about food production techniques (as indeed you may not if it's your first job and you've no prior knowledge), I've made a reasonably intelligent guess at the contents of the person specification for a machine operator. So the finished person specification might look something like this:

PERSON SPECIFICATION

MACHINE OPERATOR

E = Essential   D = Desirable

The person appointed to this post must be:

1. Fit and healthy	E
2. Attentive to detail	E
3. Observant	E
4. Clean and tidy	E
5. Thorough in their approach to their work	E
6. Able to use initiative	E
7. Reliable	E
8. Experienced in this type of work	D

'I spend a lot of time working on an application form, usually several hours spread over two or three days. It must work – I always get invited to interview.'

Quote from an employee

Now it's your turn.

Activity

Here is an advertisement and job description for a training officer. Using the process described above, work out the likely person specification.

STAFF TRAINING OFFICER

Housing and Social Services

We are looking for a suitably qualified graduate to join our small lively team involved in developing our human resource.

Broxbridge has a high commitment to staff development. New legislation, alterations in the structure of the department and changes in working practices mean that we seek an additional training officer to assist in staff training in a wide range of subjects. We seek someone with human resource qualifications, and preferably with some training experience.

Send a CV to:

Ms. D. Jones, Human Resource Manager
Broxbridge Borough Council
Room 114
Central Block
High Street
Broxbridge L11 T56

BROXBRIDGE BOROUGH COUNCIL
STAFF TRAINING OFFICER
JOB DESCRIPTION

Responsible to:

Scale:

Staff Group Training Manager

Grade C

Main purpose of job

The Staff Training Officer is responsible to the staff Group Training Manager for assisting Senior Staff Training Officers in the provision of training and development for all members of staff.

Duties

1. To analyse the training and development needs of individual members of staff and staff groups.

2. To assist in the design and delivery of appropriate training courses and development strategies to meet these needs.

3. To identify training provided out of house and to keep staff informed of such opportunities.

4. To evaluate the effectiveness of training provided both internally and externally.

5. To stock and catalogue a library of resource material for the training department.

6. To undertake any other duties as identified by the Staff Group Training Manager.

How did you get on? Did you consider general issues that you might have known from simply being aware of what's going on around you? For example, as well as more obvious items, the person specification for this particular job is likely to include something about a commitment to equal opportunities and cultural inclusiveness training and the candidate being prepared to work in a non-smoking environment.

Because these are the requirements of many councils, it makes sense to slip these details somewhere in your CV. Even if they are not on the actual person specification they would be welcomed.

Just to remind you – person specifications are usually divided into 'essential' and 'desirable' qualities. If you do have to write your own person specification, try to work out which would be which and ensure that you try to prove that you can meet at least the essential requirements. But again, don't be put off applying just because you don't have everything.

OK, so now you have all that you need to get down to work. Let's start with the easy bit.

> *'I interviewed one young woman who I felt was really special. She'd taken a year out before college and gone to Australia, then she'd gone to Africa and ended up living in a rural African village where she was the only white woman. She told me her experiences and it was clear she was very mature and had a lot of the skills we would like. I'm so glad I interviewed her, but she hadn't used any of this very relevant experience on her CV so I could easily have missed speaking to her.'*

Quote from a manager interviewing for a child care worker

Factual details

There are certain facts about you that you should always include on a CV. These are:

- your full name

- your full address including postcode

- your telephone number, including STD code, or a contact number if you don't have a phone of your own, your email address if you have one.

Date of birth

If you think that the employer might think you're too young for the job, leave out your date of birth. The reality is though, that because you won't have enough work experience to leave some out, they'll probably be able to work out your age from the dates of your jobs.

Health

You don't need to state your health on your CV if you would prefer not to, but you will almost certainly be asked this on an application form. If you have good health, state 'excellent' (anything less, even 'good' and people will think there is something wrong). The chapter on overcoming common problems discusses in more detail how to present health difficulties that need to be disclosed.

Nationality

Some people also add details of nationality. Legally, employers must be confident that you are able to work in this country and may well ask at interview to see your passport, birth certificate or work visa. However, on your CV you can choose whether or not to add nationality. If you think that your nationality may lead to unfair discrimination, leave it out.

Marital status

It is not common to put your marital status on a CV because in some cases it can lead to unfair discrimination. I recommend you leave this out.

Career objective

If you are sending your CV out 'on spec' (not in response to a specific advertisement but in the hope that the organisation will have a job of interest to you), you can state your 'career objective' under your factual information. Examples might be:

'A conscientious, hardworking person with strong communication skills. I am seeking a career in the care field.'

'A meticulous person who enjoys working alone and as part of a team, I am seeking work in the accounting field.'

'An outgoing, friendly person, I am seeking work in sales.'

Layout of factual details

Here is an example of how to present this information:

PHILLIPA RUDONISKY

123 Peterson Road

Walmsley

Lancs, WM2 3ER

01333 678903

D.o.b. 16 June 1985

'Weirdly enough, quite a lot of people actually put the time of their birth as well as the date. Do they think I'm going to do their horoscope to help me decide who to interview?'

Quote from a personnel manager

Personal profile statement

At the beginning of your CV, immediately below your name and address section, you should write a punchy personal profile statement. This is a brief statement about yourself that lets the reader have a really powerful idea of the person you are and makes them think, 'Yes! This person I want to see!'

This is where you sell all those intangible aspects of your personality that make you so great to employ. You've already given evidence of them, now's your chance to name them and sell them blatantly.

If you have any work experience your statement should start by stating who you are in work terms – 'Efficient secretary', 'Experienced machine worker' and so on. Then you write about personality traits, very important to employees. In his book *Hiring the Best* (Thorsons, 1988), John Martin Yates lists the 17 personality traits of a successful employee. Here is his list:

Personal traits

Drive: Has a desire to get things done; is goal- rather than task-oriented; has an ability to make decisions and to avoid 'busy work'; breaks overwhelming tasks into their component parts.

Motivation: Looks for new challenges; has enthusiasm and a willingness to ask questions; can motivate others through their own interests in doing a good job.

Communication: Can talk and write to people at all levels (an increasingly important skill).

Chemistry: Does not get rattled and point the finger of blame; wears a smile; has confidence without self-importance; is co-operative with others; demonstrates leadership by an ability to draw a team together.

Energy: Always gives that extra effort in the small things as well as the important tasks.

Determination: Does not back off when the going gets tough; has the ability to cope; can be assertive when necessary; is, at the same time, shrewd enough to know when it is time to back off.

Confidence: Is not ostentatious; is poised, friendly, honest with all employees, high and low, yet knows when to keep a secret.

Professional traits

Reliability: Follows up on self; does not rely on others to ensure that a job is well done; keeps management informed.

Integrity: Takes responsibility for own actions, whether good or bad; makes decisions in the best interests of the company, not on their own whim or personal preference.

Dedication: Has a commitment to tasks and projects; does what is necessary to see a project through to completion on deadline.

Pride: Has pride in trade or profession; takes the extra step and always pays attention to details to see the job is done to the best of ability.

Analytical skills: Weighs the pros and cons; does not jump at the first solution that presents itself; analyses the short- and long-term benefits of a solution against all its possible negatives; possesses the perception and insight that lead to good judgement.

Listening skills: Listens and understands rather than waits for a chance to speak; has attentiveness that complements analytical skills.

Business traits

Efficiency: Always keeps an eye open for wastes of time, effort, resources, and money.

Economy: Knows the difference between expensive and cheap solutions to problems; spends your money as if it were his or her own.

Procedures: Knows that procedures usually exist for good reason, and won't work around them; has a willingness to keep you informed; follows the chain of command; does not implement own 'improved' procedures or organise others to do so.

Profit: Knows it's the reason we're all here.

Activity

1. Make a list of the personality traits that you think apply to you and what examples you can provide if you get to interview. Keep in mind that much of your evidence will be amply demonstrated by the 'noteworthy extras' you have listed above. However, it is possible that you can give an example from some other area of your CV, such as the interests section.

2. Think about those traits you would like to develop. What steps can you take to achieve them? Write a step-by-step approach to make sure you develop and keep these traits.

'One person actually wrote 'I think I'm assertive, but my daughter says I'm bossy!' This may have been an amusing thing to say at interview, but it's definitely not the sort of thing to write on an application form or CV.'

Quote from a manager

Here is an example of a personal profile prepared by an applicant for the training officer job we looked at a while back:

Staff and management development professional. I work well with staff at all levels. Energetic and enthusiastic; I have experience in running a wide range of staff development courses. I am also computer literate, competent on several software packages.

and one for the night shift worker's vacancy:

> Experienced worker with excellent attention to detail. Knowledge of hygiene regulations and food production techniques.

and one for a mechanic:

> A practical, skilled mechanic with a positive attitude and sound diagnostic skills.

Here is a handy format for writing your profile:

'A ...(describe your first personality quality using an adjective)... (second positive personality adjective)... (describe your present situation, e.g. student or job title),... with strong/ excellent/outstanding/exceptional skills in ... (skill area). My experience has provided me with the following strengths:

- Strength one
- Strength two
- Strength three
- Strength four
- Strength five
- Strength six

If you are writing 'on spec' you may also like to add 'seeking... (type of work you are looking for)'.

As in the format above, you can follow up this profile with some bullet points highlighting your strengths. Add a sentence that says something like 'I also have the following strengths, skills and qualities' or 'My career to date has given me the following strengths, abilities and qualities'. Follow this with six or eight bullet points (dots, stars, whatever) emphasising these aspects of your abilities. Examples might be:

- conscientious
- adaptable

- hardworking

- energetic

- highly motivated

- enthusiastic.

An alternative way of showing 'personality' information

If your professional profile box at the top of your CV is fairly full with factual detail you may wish to tell the shortlister about your wonderful personality elsewhere. This could come under the heading of 'Other information'. The next section features other items to include under this heading, but if you choose to use this section to 'sell' your personality make it as punchy and descriptive as you can. As the interviewer at the beginning of this chapter said, let the reader know the sort of person they can expect to see sitting in front of them if they offer you an interview. Here are some examples.

'I am a reliable and enthusiastic worker. I enjoy working with others and can work well without supervision.'

'I am a punctual and dependable person. I am used to working under tight deadlines and enjoy a challenge.'

'I am very enthusiastic about working with computers and have received a lot of positive feedback about my ability to teach software packages.'

'I enjoy working with people. I believe I am a good listener and am sympathetic to the needs of young children and their parents.'

'Experienced model-maker, excellent at precision work. Good liaison and team-working skills.'

'Enthusiastic trainee mechanic with considerable practical experience.'

'Experienced and enthusiastic group leader, highly committed to helping others work towards a common goal.'

Education and training information

There are actually two headings here – 'Education' and 'Training'. Depending on your own circumstances you might choose to separate the information or put them together under different headings. Whichever way you choose, here are a few tips to help you present the information in the best possible way.

Education information

Education information consists of three groups of information – where you attended school/college, when and the qualifications you obtained.

- No employer is likely to be interested in details of your primary school so don't include this information.

- Don't give the whole address of secondary schools or college; simply 'St John's School, Bradford' is enough.

- Remember to be consistent in the way you present information.

- If you are writing a list of, say, exam passes, put the most relevant ones at the top.

The higher up the educational ladder you go, the less you need to mention lower qualifications, so if you:

- only have five GCSEs mention each one separately. Also, if you are a school-leaver you would normally add the grades you achieved (though if they are poor you might want to omit them)

- if you have a degree, you probably wouldn't bother to list the GCSEs unless there was a good reason to do so.

> *'You'd be surprised how many people write their whole address under 'Place of Birth'. Anyone would think we need to know that they were born in Flat 2, 27 High Street. Tell people they only need to write the town (and country if out of the UK).'*

> **Quote from a personnel manager**

Here is an example of how to present education information:

Jennifer Ann Peters

26 Sunningdale Road
Marlsham
Norfolk
NR2 6AS

01990 575849

Date of Birth 26.2.1986

Schools attended:

2002–2004   Berne Community College, Marsham

1997–2002   St Mary's School, Oxford

Qualifications

2004   GCE A level: English B   Sociology C

2002   GCSE:

English B	Mathematics C	Geography A
History C	Art A	Sociology B
Design C		

Training information

The term training covers a multitude of different teaching methods. For example you may have attended short courses or a longer course that are not certificated. You may have some NVQ or GNVQ units. You could have done an apprenticeship or attended an in-company course. Less formally, you could have been coached by other members of staff, spent time in different departments or attended evening classes.

Any, or all of these, are likely to be of interest to a potential employer. Some people are course junkies and soon collect quite a long list. If this applies to you, be selective about which ones to include. Ignore courses that have no direct relevance to the job you are applying for. The link, by the way, could be that the course (perhaps recreational) highlights some personal characteristic that will be useful for the work. If so, try to spell this out, perhaps in the 'Additional information' section, or the reader may not understand the point.

Here are some tips about presenting 'training' information:

- List your courses in the best possible order – by relevance to the job and by standard.

- If the course title leaves the reader unclear as to its content, *very briefly* state what was included, perhaps by listing the modules.

- If the course is a long one but still did not lead to a qualification, state the length of the course or the reader may think it's just another short course.

- State where you did the course, but don't put the whole address. Simply 'Cambridge Regional College' or 'Timeworks, London'.

Do remember to consider transferable skills when you are deciding which courses to include in your list. For example, suppose you worked in a shop and the company sent you on a 'customer service' course. The skills you learn on that course would be just as valuable if you became a sales rep, a customer services manager, work in a different type of shop or indeed anywhere else where you have direct contact with customers.

Activity

Make a note of your education and training details. Remember to include date, school/college attended, brief address, qualification and grades (if appropriate). For training include course title, date, training organisation and content if appropriate.

Work experience/career to date/career history

This section usually takes the longest to compose because you are carefully matching your information against the items in the job description and person specification for the job. You will see that I have given three titles here – use whichever you prefer or another similar one of your choice.

The prospective employer will read through the education section of your CV, and briefly note if you've got the right qualifications, but this is the section they will scrutinise most closely. Therefore time taken here is well spent.

If you have worked your way through the chapter on self-analysis you will have already done most of the work needed. If you haven't go back now and work through the material so that you have an accurate assessment of all your skills and an idea of how to use words to best effect.

Before you consider how to present this information remember that it should be woven into the fabric of your work experience. There are a number of different ways to show work experience on a CV and we'll look at these later in the chapter.

Activity

1. In your notebook, list all your work experience. Remember to include holiday jobs, part-time work, full-time work, voluntary work, work experience/shadowing.

2. Then, under each heading, notes your dates – from start of employment to finish (month and year is sufficient).

3. Now take each of the jobs in turn and make a list of the responsibilities you held in the job. These are likely to be much the same as the job description if you were given one at the time. Take into account any additional responsibilities – most jobs develop over time as the needs of the organisation or the interests of the employee shape them.

4. Now for each of these jobs ask yourself 'What did I do that was noteworthy?' These are the special things you noted in Chapter four – *Evidence of Success*.

When you are writing your 'career to date' section, weave into your statements those words that you have underlined as being significant in the job description and person specification of the job you are applying for. This will work on the shortlister unconsciously and help them to feel well disposed towards your application.

'The first thing the interviewer said to me was "We were very impressed by your CV". It helped me to feel good straight away.'

Quote from a receptionist

OK, so now you have job titles, factual details about them – date, etc. responsibilities in each job and noteworthy 'extras' for each job.

Strictly speaking, that is all you need for the 'Career to date' section. As you list the responsibilities of each job, ensure that they are shown in the same order as in the job description (assuming you have the necessary experience). This makes it easier for the shortlister to check that you meet their requirements.

An example of how to list the responsibilities of the job under the title is shown here:

2001-2004 Training Manager, Insurance Industries Ltd, Rotherham

In this busy post I have responsibility for:

- training and development needs of 650 staff

- analysis of training needs

- design and delivery of training courses

- appointing external trainers and other recruitment tasks

- allocation of training budget.

Whilst in post I have completed an extensive training needs analysis and provided training linked to company objectives. All were within budget. I have also provided a library of management and related books for staff use.

Other information

As with the factual information, there is a choice of layouts and headings for the odds and ends you still want to include but which haven't fitted neatly within any of the previous headings. Your information may fit into one of the following headings.

1. Leisure interests

2. Additional information

3. Publications

4. References

Leisure interests

It is more or less expected that you will include a section under this heading, although you may choose to use the heading 'Additional information' if that feels more appropriate (for example, if you want to include both leisure interests and information about one of the other items in this section).

Additional information

The type of additional information that may well interest a prospective employer (or college) would be:

- membership of a club

- membership of a debating society

- extra responsibilities at school or college

- involvement with a charity or fundraising organisation

- playing sports

- voluntary work

- Duke of Edinburgh Award.

Having said that, some of these activities may well have provided you with experience that you can emphasise in the body of your CV.

If you decide to use one of the headings suggested above, don't just list the items. Think instead about what might interest the employer. Going through the above list I could easily identify:

- **Membership of a club** can indicate that you are a sociable person, or if the club is based around an interest or skill that you are good at whatever that is. Shows that you are not too much of a loner.

- **Membership of a debating society** indicates an ability to present yourself verbally, to think through issues logically and calmly.

- **Extra responsibilities at school or college** (for example, being a prefect) shows that you are reliable, trustworthy, respected, etc.

- **Playing sports** shows that you are fit. Playing a team sport shows that you can work as a member of a team, play by the rules, etc.

- **Voluntary work** shows that you like to help others less fortunate than yourself. Shows reliability, initiative, etc.

- **Duke of Edinburgh Award** shows many positive attributes depending on what you've covered, but including staying power, reliability and willingness to work hard.

Providing this information to prospective employers is especially important if you are a school or college leaver with no work experience to offer as proof of your abilities.

Publications

If you've been fortunate enough to have something published, no matter how modest the publication, do mention it. The format is:

Title   *Journal/Publisher*   *Date of Publication*

Generally, the titles of articles are shown in plain type with quotation marks and the title of books are shown in italic type.

Maybe you haven't written a book or article but have written something else useful. Have you designed web pages? Written an information leaflet? Edited the school magazine? All of these would be of interest to an employer. If any relate directly to the type of work you are applying for, you may want to send a copy or give a brief description.

References

It is entirely up to you to decide whether or not to provide details of referees on your CV. If you are applying for a specific job, it is helpful to include this information because some organisations insist on having the reference in front of them prior to the interview.

If, however, you are sending a CV out uninvited there is no need to include this information unless you particularly want to. The organisation can always ask for details of referees if they contact you for interview.

When you do provide this information choose your referees carefully. You should select people who you feel have a good opinion of you and who know something about you in the capacity you are seeking. Do check with them that they will be willing to provide a reference. It sometimes happens that people get letters requesting a reference on someone they feel is totally unsuitable for the job in question and this can be very embarrassing. Much better to check it out first. If the person agrees to provide a reference, do tell them about the job so that they have a chance to think about it ahead of time. Check too that they won't be away on holiday at the crucial time.

The information referees receive with the request varies. Some organisations simply ask referees to 'Write about the suitability of the person' without giving much guidance. Some ask referees to complete a form. Others send the job description and person specification and ask for comments in relation to these documents. Others phone.

It is usual to supply the names, addresses and telephone numbers of two referees. Obviously if you have had a previous job, one of your referees should be your previous manager. If you have not had a previous job you could ask:

- a teacher from school or lecturer from college

- a professional person who knows you well

- the chairperson or leader of a club you belong to

- a family friend who has a professional job.

If you are already employed and don't want your present employer to know that you are applying for other jobs, mention this in your covering letter (some application forms ask the question anyway). Simply say something like, 'Please do not contact my employer for a reference unless a job offer is to be made.'

Writing a CV to send out speculatively

So far we have been talking about CVs that are written specifically to apply for a particular job. You may decide that you want to send your CV to several organisations 'on spec'.

Many people hesitate to do this, but what have you got to lose but your time and the cost of the stationery and stamps? Remember, many organisations are delighted to be able to fill posts without the expense and trouble of advertising.

There are three approaches to sending out CVs speculatively.

1. You send your CV to every organisation you can think of that may have a vacancy. This would work, for example, for a typist job – almost every organisation has some office staff.

2. You send your CV to the types of organisation that may possibly have specific types of work – for example, all building companies in your area if you're looking for a bricklaying job.

3. You send out your CV to organisations that have been in the news and that you think may therefore have an opening in future. This would be the case, for example, if you read that a company had won a big contract, is expanding, or has received an award. Anything positive, in fact, might be worth following with a CV and a covering letter. The chapter on covering letters gives information on what to write in these circumstances.

The advantages of sending a CV 'on spec' are:

■ it shows the organisation that you are self motivated and can use your initiative

■ even if there is not a vacancy at the moment, your information may be kept on file and the organisation will contact you if a vacancy arises

■ you may catch the organisation at a time when a vacancy has just arisen and they have not yet had an opportunity to advertise

■ you may contact the organisation when they are considering starting a new post – you'll be first in the queue

■ you could even find yourself being the only one interviewed because the organisation has not advertised the vacancy, which means that as long as you're good you don't have to worry about other interviewees who might be even better…

To sum up.

■ Think about the sort of work you want to apply for.

■ Work out what the job entails and try to write your own job description and person specification.

■ Write your CV as if you were writing to the organisation for that job.

■ Write a suitable covering letter, indicating exactly the type of work you seek, or saying that you are open to suggestions. Alternatively, you could say that you are really looking for X job but would be willing to consider others.

■ Find out the name of the personnel or relevant manager and send your letter and CV direct to that person (again, this shows initiative and will only cost a phone call).

■ Consider following up your mailing with a phone call a few days later. If you do this, prepare beforehand for the call: what are you going to say? Make a few notes to ensure you handle the call well.

Activity

Investigate all the organisations in your area (or the area in which you would like to live) which would have the type of vacancy you are looking for. Remember to find out to whom CVs should be sent.

Useful web addresses for CV writing advice

Sites with good advice and sample CVs:

www.alec.co.uk/CVtips

www.handsoncv.co.uk/homepage.asp – a site where you can complete a blank CV on-line. Sample CVs available to view.

www.jobstar.org/ – again, an American site with lots of job search advice.

Scannable CVs

Some organisations will scan your CV using specialist software. If they receive many applications this will save them time reading through all of them. They may request that you present your CV in a particular way, showing bare essentials or they may scan the CV just as you send it.

The software will be looking for key words or phrases in your CV, chosen because they are considered of most importance in the potential postholder. Key words might include 'motivated', 'hardworking', 'good communicator', 'dynamic', etc. If you follow the advice throughout this chapter and ensure that you construct your CV in such a way that it includes key words from the job description, person specification and advertisement, you won't go far wrong. Take into account also John Martin Yate's key personality traits on page 96.

If you are asked for a scannable CV but not given a template, keep these points in mind.

1. Put your name at the top of each page on a line with nothing else on it.

2. Write all contact details on separate lines with no punctuation marks.

3. Use a single column format as OCRs read from left to right.

4. Use **Bold** or CAPITALS for headings. Keep it simple, don't use borders, italics, underlining, shading or anything else that may confuse the scanner and prevent a good reading.

5. Use a sans serif font such as Ariel or Helvetica that is easy to read, ideally 12pt and definitely not less than 10pt.

6. Leave some space between sections.

7. Leave spaces between slashes, e.g. three / four.

8. Ensure your CV is printed on white, good quality paper using a laser printer.

9. Don't fax your CV as the quality will not be good enough to scan.

10. Send your CV unfolded and unstapled as either can cause misreading of the text.

11. Do not include anything that might confuse the software. This includes ampersands, hollow bullet points, currency symbols, unusual graphics and foreign characters.

12. Always spell check.

13. If emailing your CV, save it as a PlainText document, and attach the text file to your email message/covering letter.

Chapter checklist

In this chapter we have looked at what needs to go into your CV. Some points to consider are:

■   always give yourself plenty of time to prepare your CV

■   gather all the information you need before you start

■   study all the information available about the job and organisation

■   underline/highlight those words that are most important

■   always start by thinking about what the shortlister is looking for

- mould your writing to the employer's stated needs (or what you think they are)

- use lots of positive words

- really sell your successes

- remember to show yourself as a 'balanced' person

- if no suitable job openings appear, consider sending your CV out 'on 'spec'.

Chapter eight
CV layout options

You should read this chapter:

- when you have gathered together all the information you wish to include in a CV.

By the end of this chapter you should know:

- the variety of ways in which a CV can be presented

- the advantages and disadvantages of each format

- which format will best suit your purpose

- what steps to take if you decide to send out your CV 'speculatively'.

CV options

There is no single 'correct' way to present a CV and this allows you to express your own creativity through your layout. However, there are certain conventions that should be followed. The exception to this would be if you are applying for a creative job where a more adventurous approach might demonstrate your abilities.

Electronic CVs

Some employers advertise for staff on the web (see Chapter one for more details). And some of them are now adding CV templates so that you can send your CV direct by email. The advice given in this chapter will help you to make the most of whatever template you encounter.

Templates on your PC

Wordprocessing packages offer a variety of PC templates and you might like to look at those before you start your CV to see if you think any of them will suit you. You should be able to complete any of them using the information in this chapter.

Chronological CV

As the name suggests, a chronological CV presents material in chronological (date) order *in reverse* – that is, most recent information is shown first. The chronological CV takes the reader step by step through your education history, then your work history and finally to your additional information.

In graphic form, the chronological CV looks like this:

Name
Address
Telephone
(Mobile)
email address
Date of birth

Professional profile *(see Chapter seven for details of how to write this)*

Education and Training

Dates	Names of schools
	Details of exams

Career to date

Dates	Name and address of employer
	Job title
	Responsibilities in that job
	Any 'extras' you can claim

Additional information

This can be anything you think the employer may be interested in. Belonging to clubs and societies for example or doing a Duke of

---

Edinburgh Award or helping run a Brownie pack. Anything you do that you think demonstrates skills or personal qualities that the employer might be looking for.

Interests

Even within this format, there is a choice of how to present information. Remember, there are several ways to do this; choose whichever you prefer. The golden rule is MAKE IT EASY FOR THE READER TO ABSORB THE INFORMATION YOU PROVIDE. This means presenting your information attractively and consistently.

The advantages of the chronological CV are that it is the one most employers are familiar with. They can find out a lot about you if they read this type of CV carefully – information such as whether you have any career gaps, etc. Chronological CVs also fill a page which is useful if you are young and don't yet have much experience to offer and therefore not much to write about.

Also this type of CV provides a useful reference guide to you for future CVs and indeed application forms.

The only disadvantage is that it can be a fairly bland predictable read for a prospective interviewer.

But don't do this...

There is one 'wrong' way to write a CV and that is to mix styles. Look at this example:

CURRICULUM VITAE

Phillipa Rudinsky,
123 Peterson Road,
Walmsley
Lancs
WM2 3ER
01333 568991
email philippa@robins.net

16 June 1985

Education and Training

Sept 1996 - June 2001	Collett Community College, Warmsley Qualifications: GCSE

English	B
Maths	D
textiles	C
Business Studies	A
geography	C

Sept 2001 - July 2002	Walmsley Regional College Qualifications: City & Guilds Catering NVQ level 1
	Royal Inst of Public Health – Foundation Certificate in Food Hygiene
Sept 2002 - July 2004	Walmsley Regional College Qualification: BTEC National Diploma in Care
2.9.2002 - to present	Walmsley Regional College Level 1 Certificate Text Processing (part-time)

Career to date

Part-time work, while at school or college

N.A.S. Newsagents, Victoria Lane, Walmsley

July 2000 - February 2001

Saturday position involving handling money, dealing with customers, sorting out paper bills, and shelf filing.

Bakers Food Shops, Arthur Street, Walmsley 3.3.2002 - 3.9.2002

This job involved handling money, helping customers, filling shelves and working as part of a team.

Jane Pearce Elderly People's Home, Fortescue Road, Walmsley

Sept 2002 – March 2004

I worked at Jane Pearce House in the kitchens as a weekend cook to support me through college. This involved the ability to supervise others, devise and cook menus as well as prepare the evening tea.

Full-time work since leaving college

> **Jane Pearce Elderly People's Home, Fortescue Road, Walmsley**
>
> July 2004 – present
>
> Care Assistant. This responsible role involved caring for elderly people, ambulance escort duty, collecting and banking money and the supervision of others.
>
> **Other information**
>
> I enjoy working and being with others. I also enjoy swimming, needlepoint and dancing. I am a keen cook and like to experiment in the

Can you spot the deliberate mistakes?

- Inconsistent use of commas at the end of lines in the address (tip – don't use any, it's not current business practice)

- Inconsistent method of presenting dates, e.g. 2.9.2002 and Sept 2002 – make sure you use the same system throughout

- GCSEs – inconsistent use of capital letters

- Spelling mistake – shelf 'filling' not 'filing'

- Inconsistent use of underlining and bold to emphasise words

- Not all the jobs show the job title even though it is implied by the type of work undertaken. They should always be shown.

Skills-based (or functional) CV

As the name suggests, this CV presentation is written to emphasise skills rather than take the reader chronologically through the life of the writer. This is an increasingly popular form of CV presentation, although it does require that you already have relevant skills or you'll find it difficult to fill a page!

To write a skills-based CV you simply do the same preparation as before, linking your skills with the job requirements. Then you present your skills in a punchy and eye-catching way. They are the main emphasis of this layout.

As you will see from the examples that follow, this type of CV does not state which skills have been used in which job. A skills-based CV often fits on one side of A4 paper.

Here are some examples of the format of this type of CV:

Name
Address
Telephone
Date of birth

Professional Profile

Education (brief details only)

Capabilities

- list them here by using bullet points

Achievements

- again, list them here using bullet points

Career History

for each job list brief details of:

- employer's name and short address
- dates of employment
- job title

Additional information

(Unless you decide to provide this information in your covering letter)

or alternatively:

Name

Address

Telephone

Date of birth

Professional Profile

Education (brief details only)

One skill area

- list skills under this heading using bullet points

Another skills area

- as before, list skills using bullet points
- continue until you have shown all your relevant skills

Career to date

- for each job list brief details of:

  - employer's name and short address

  - dates of employment

  - job title

Additional information

(Unless you decide to provide this information in your covering letter)

Collette's chronological CV

I'm assuming for this CV (see overleaf) that Collette is looking for a secretarial job and is sending her CV out 'on spec' to a number of local companies. Note that she has stated at the top of the CV the type of work she is looking for. She would, of course, also mention this in her covering letter.

How do you think Collette comes across? She is clearly a lively and enterprising person who enjoys being with others. She has a good range of exam passes relevant to the work she seeks. Additionally, she has managed to pass these whilst still taking on the work with the drama

Collette Hay
27 Blinco Road
Wareham
Lancs LA5 8MM

01333 787878

Date of birth 16.12.1987

Job Target: Administrative or secretarial post

Professional Profile

A conscientious and hardworking school-leaver with up-to-date secretarial skills.

Career History

June 2004 – Aug 2004

> Hurst's Office Supplies Ltd, High Street, Wareham LA5 2NP.
> Administrative Assistant

- typing letters and invoices
- filing
- answering the telephone
- relief reception work

Vacation Work

July 2003 – present

> St Joseph's Home, Dear St, Wareham LA5 5NT.
> Day Care Assistant

- working with a variety of professionals
- dealing with a variety of personal needs of the residents
- writing diary notes on each resident
- dealing with the relatives of residents
- taking part in outings, etc.

Whilst working at St. Joseph's I invented a new board game for the residents which has proved very popular.

Education

1999-2004   St Joseph's Comprehensive, Wareham

GCSE

English   B
Mathematics   A
Geography   C
History   E
Art   A
Business Studies   B

OCR Level 1 Certificate in Text Processing

Additional information

For the past two years I have been secretary of the school drama club. This has given me a wide range of secretarial experience from taking minutes of meetings to handling monies from ticket sales. I enjoyed working as part of the team developing each drama production and also enjoyed working alone on those aspects of my secretarial role that required this.

I am a keen photographer and also enjoy netball and swimming. I enjoy reading historical novels.

References

Mrs Jane Briggs, Manager   Mr John Oman
Hurst's Office Supplies   7 Aubray Road
High Street   Wareham
Wareham   Lancs LA5 4SN
Lancs LA5 2NP   (family friend)

group and following her other hobbies. Most employers with a suitable vacancy would think she is a person worth seeing after reading this CV. Added to that, she has shown considerable initiative in sending it out 'on spec'.

Now we'll see how the CV looks with another format.

Collette's skill-based CV

Collette Hay
27 Blinco Road
Wareham
Lancs LA5 8MM

01333 787878

Date of birth 16.12.1987

Job Target: Administrative or secretarial post

Professional Profile

A conscientious and hardworking school-leaver with up-to-date secretarial skills.

Abilities

- typing letters and invoice
- filing
- answering the telephone
- reception work
- message-taking
- working with people at all levels

Career to date

July 2003 – present (vacation work)	St Joseph's Home, Dear St, Wareham LA5 5NT Day Care Assistant
June 2004 – Aug 2004	Hurst's Office Supplies Ltd, High Street, Wareham LA5 2NP Administrative Assistant

Qualifications

2004: 6 GCSEs – English B, Mathematics A, Geography C, History E, Art A, Business Studies B
OCR Level 1 Certificate in Text Processing

Additional information

I am a conscientious and hard-working person who enjoys working as part of a team, but am also well motivated to work unsupervised. I pay good attention to detail and enjoy working to deadlines.

I am a keen photographer and also enjoy netball and swimming. I am an enthusiastic reader of historical novels.

Put yourself in the shoes of the shortlister. She or he is looking for people who can meet those criteria outlined on the job description and person specification. The skills-based CV does save time checking skills, because they don't have to be hunted for in with a lot of other information.

Spacing

As we've seen earlier, one rule on CV presentation is that you don't use more than two sides of A4 paper. As a school or college leaver you may find it difficult to fill two sides. Collette's skills-based CV, when presented on A4 paper, might fill only one side. If it goes over to the second page she would have to make a decision either to space out the work so that it fills the second page, or to squash it up a bit to get it on one page.

Don't worry if the whole of page two isn't full, if necessary just send a one page CV. If you decide to, you can 'squeeze' or 'expand' your information by:

- having bigger or smaller margins

- leaving more or less space between each heading

- listing examination results under or next to each other

- writing any addresses over one or more lines

- putting in, or leaving out, the words 'Curriculum Vitae'

- putting the referees' names and addresses under or next to each other.

CV for a second job

James wants to apply for a job as trainee manager with a nationwide white goods store.

James's chronological CV

CURRICULUM VITAE

James Matthew Whiteways
27 High Meadows, Thornton, Derbyshire DE13 1AH
01234 4455662
1.2.1984
Health: Excellent

Professional Profile

An enthusiastic and successful retail salesperson with experience of selling electrical equipment and stock control systems.

Career to date

2000 – present   Salesperson, Hodder Electrical Ltd, Highgate Shopping Centre, Thornton

- Specialist knowledge of stereo systems and video recorders and cameras

- Responsibility for stock control when manager away

During the past year at Hodder Electrical Ltd I have increased sales in the stereo and video department by 15%.

1999 – 2000   Campbell's Shoes Ltd, Twenty Street, Thornton Salesperson (Saturdays and vacation)

1998-1999   The Corner Shop, 23 Garden Road, Thornton Newspaper delivery

Education and Training

2001   Effective Selling Skills. Three-day, in-house course.

1995 – 2000   Wells Community College, Thornton
GCSE

English	Grade B
Maths	Grade C
Art	Grade C
History	Grade E
Geography	Grade D
French	Grade E

Interests

I am an enthusiastic footballer and a member of Thornton Sports and Social Club Committee where I have responsibility for social activities. I enjoy reading thrillers and socialising with friends.

James's skills-based CV

James Matthew Whiteways
27 High Meadows, Thornton, Derbyshire DE13 1HA
01234 4455662
1.2.1984
Health: Excellent

Professional Profile

An enthusiastic and successful retail salesperson with experience of selling electrical equipment and stock control systems.

Capabilities

- Knowledge of white goods of all sorts
- Specialist knowledge of video and stereo systems and cameras
- Managing stock control systems
- Working to target
- Excellent customer care
- Working knowledge of wordprocessing

Accomplishments

Increased sales in video and stereo department by 15% in one year

Career History

2000 – present	Salesperson, Hodder Electrical Ltd, Highgate Shopping Centre, Thornton
1999 – 2000	Campbell's Shoes Ltd, Twenty Street, Thornton Salesperson (Saturdays and vacation)
1998-1999	The Corner Shop, 23 Garden Road, Thornton Newspaper delivery

Education and Training

Effective Sales Skills – three-day, in-house course

6 GCSEs including English and Maths

Additional information

I am a highly motivated and successful salesperson who enjoys working as part of a team. I am presentable and relate well to customers. I find that staff often turn to me for advice on a variety of matters.

I am an enthusiastic footballer and a member of Thornton Sports and Social Club Committee where I have responsibility for social activities. I enjoy reading thrillers and socialising with friends.

CV for graduates with some work experience

Sally is a graduate with work experience. She is applying for a job as a researcher with a pressure group working for reform of the prison system. Both her chronological and skills-based CV follow. Spend a few minutes comparing the two. Consider jobs you might apply for and decide which CV would suit your needs best.

Sally Jane Dowling
27 Upper North Street
Dainow
DN23 6PB
01229 868686
22.10.1980

Professional Profile

An energetic and enthusiastic researcher with experience of working in penal reform. My experience and education mean that I can offer the following skills and abilities:

- excellent attention to detail
- knowledge of criminal justice
- self motivated
- qualitative and quantitative research experience
- good team worker
- excellent communication skills

Career to date

1999-2001   North East London Probation Service
Probation Assistant
In this busy post I was responsible for:

- interviewing probationers
- writing reports
- co-leading groups
- liaising with other professionals
- attending case conferences

1998-1998   Dainow Shoe Company
Saturday Sales Assistant

- serving customers
- answering the telephone
- money handling

Education

2001-2004   BA (Hons) Social Research 2:1
University of North London

1992-1999   Dainow Comprehensive College
GCE A level: Sociology A, English B, History D
GCSEs: English, Mathematics, History, Sociology,
Geography, Religious Studies, Art

Additional information

I have a long-term interest in the field of criminology and penal reform. My dissertation at university was on 'Problems faced by prisoners' families' and won the Jane McDonald Award for best dissertation of the year.

I very much enjoyed the research element of my degree which lasted two years, and I feel enthusiastic about pursuing penal reform as a career.

I am a friendly, outgoing person and have a passion for computing. I enjoy working as part of a team, but am well motivated to work on my own.

Leisure interests

I am a bit of a film buff and enjoy old movies as well as current releases. I belong to a squash club where I play regularly. I love reading, especially family novels and suspense.

... and now a skills-based version:

Sally Jane Dowling
27 Upper North Street
Dainow
DN23 6PB
01229 868686
22.10.1980

Professional Profile

An energetic and enthusiastic researcher with experience of working in penal reform.

Education

2004   B.A. (Hons.) Social Research 2:1
                              University of North London

Capabilities

Research experience

- Problems faced by prisoners' families; qualitative research
- Evaluation of effectiveness of groups in probation
- Two years study of research methods in BA

Writing

- Writing up research findings
- Writing reports
- Writing diary records and group and case work

Communicating

- Liaising with a wide range of professionals
- Attending case conferences
- Dealing with a variety of clients
- Working as part of a probation team
- Interviewing prisoners' families

Computing

- MS Office
- SSAS research package
- Publisher

Employment

1999-2001 North East London Probation Service, Probation Assistant

1998-1998 Dainow Shoe Company, Saturday Sales Assistant

Achievements

I won the Jane McDonald Award at university for best dissertation in my year.

Additional information

I have a long term interest in the field of criminology and penal reform. My dissertation at university was on 'Problems faced by prisoners' families' and won the Jane McDonald Award for best dissertation of the year. I very much enjoyed the research element of my degree which lasted two years, and I feel enthusiastic about pursuing penal reform as a career.

I am a friendly, outgoing person and have a passion for computing. I enjoy working as part of a team, but am well motivated to work on my own.

Leisure interests

I am a bit of a film buff and enjoy old movies as well as current releases. I belong to squash club where I play regularly. I love reading, especially family novels and suspense.

In the skills-based version Sally may have chosen to leave out the 'Additional information' and to include it in her covering letter instead. The fact that Sally had won an award for an outstanding dissertation as an undergraduate would be of great interest to a prospective employer. It is well worth, therefore, including it under a heading of 'Achievements'.

If you choose a skills-based format for your CV this could be where you provide information on those things you have done that are over and above what is normally expected at work or college.

Practical considerations

Here are some points to remember to ensure your CV looks attractive:

- don't make your CV look cramped; leave plenty of 'white space' around your words

- leave a good margin around your text, about 25mm

- generally use single spacing, but double between paragraphs

- if using a typewriter, make sure the ribbon doesn't need replacing

- be consistent in the way you present information – make reading as easy as possible

- use good quality paper – 80gsm at least

- always keep in mind – does this look like a document I would want to read?'

By the way, always keep some spare paper so that you can write your covering letter on the same stuff.

Chapter checklist

Do:

- be consistent in the way you present material – make is easy for the reader to shortlist you

- decide which CV style would best present the information you want to show

- make yourself come alive as a person rather than just a list of facts

- keep a copy of your CV for future reference

- consider sending out a CV speculatively, especially if there are few vacancies being advertised.

Don't:

- use more than two sheets of A4 paper

- produce the CV double sided

- use poor quality paper

- use abbreviations, especially if they might be unfamiliar to the reader

- use only one CV for everything. Write a fresh version for each job – usually you will only have to make modifications, and not have to do a complete re-write

- forget what you've written – use a copy of your CV as a crib sheet prior to interview

- assume that the reader will know what your past jobs involved

- forget which version of your CV you've sent. Make a copy and note on it which job it relates to.

Chapter nine
Sample CVs

You should read this chapter:

- when you need to prepare a CV for either a specific job or for a general mailing to a number of organisations.

By the end of this chapter you should:

- have a much clearer idea of what a range of CVs look like

- be able to select the CV for your needs.

A reminder

Do remember that the following CVs are just examples of the types of layout you might like to consider. Your own layout is up to you. Do, however, read the previous chapters to help you to make the best possible decision.

Example of a CV for a school leaver – 1

Jane Blanton
35 Birmingham Road
Solihull
BM1 3LL
0121 330 4455
dob 10.2.1987
jane.blanton@talknet.com

CAREER OBJECTIVE

A hardworking, reliable person with excellent communication skills, seeking an opportunity as a management trainee within the retail industry.

PROFILE

A self-motivated, hardworking school leaver with work experience in retail. Good customer service skills and keen to develop further abilities.

EDUCATION AND QUALIFICATIONS

1998– 2003	Marlow Comprehensive School, Plough Street, West Wickham CB4 4RR GCSE English Grade B, Maths Grade C, Geography Grade B, Design and Technology Grade A, Religious Studies Grade E, French Grade B
2003	Marlow Comprehensive Evening Centre, West Wickham French Evening Classes
Dec 2002	McGregors Customer Service Training McGregors Hygiene Training

WORK EXPERIENCE

Oct 2002   Neve's Ltd, The High Street, West Wickham CB4 1HO.

Ladies Fashion Store.

During my one-week work experience placement with Neve's, I learned how to:

- serve customers
- use the till – both cash and card transactions
- answer the phone.

Dec 2002-	McGregors, Greens Road, West Wickham CB4 8FA.
July 2003	My part-time post with McGregors has given me experience of:

- working as part of a team
- working in a high pressure, fast food environment
- ensuring that my work was hygienic at all times
- customer service
- cash handling.

ACHIEVEMENTS

In school	Member of the netball team
	Member of French conversation group

INTERESTS AND HOBBIES

My family and I go camping in France most summers and I speak French fairly well. I enjoy spending time with friends, going to the cinema and dancing. I like to read, mostly romance and crime stories.

REFERENCES

Mrs Jameson
Head Teacher
Marlow Comprehensive School
Plough Street
West Wickham
CB4 4RR

Samantha Ahmed
Manager
Neve's Ltd
The High Street
West Wickham
CB4 1HO

Example of a CV for a school leaver – 2

JONATHON EDMUNDS
33 Snetterton Road, Wellesbourne SA33 5RA

PERSONAL INFORMATION

Tel no: 01889 545470
email: j.edmunds@global.net
Date of birth: 5 February 1986

PROFILE

I am sociable, lively and have good communication skills. I get on well with most people, am renowned for keeping cool under pressure and enjoy learning new skills.

EDUCATION AND QUALIFICATIONS

2002-2004 Wellesbourne Community College, Wellesbourne SA33 3RR

NVQ level 3 in Business Studies

1997-2002 Wellesbourne Comprehensive School, Baker Street, Wellesbourne SA33 4WW

GCSEs:

English	Grade A
Maths	Grade A
History	Grade B
Social Studies	Grade B
Childcare	Grade C

WORK EXPERIENCE

2003-present   Speedy Pizza, High Street, Wellesbourne SA33 5TY.

Evening and weekend work at this busy pizza restaurant and take-away. My duties include:

- waiting at tables
- money handling
- answering the phone and taking orders
- working as part of a team.

April-May 2004   Rototech Ltd, Bullon Business Park, The Fairway, Wellesbourne.

Office Assistant – Work experience from college. My duties included:

- photocopying

- dealing with incoming and outgoing post

- entering data on database

- filing.

ACHIEVEMENTS

In school   Active member of Wellesbourne Community College Student Union

In college   Made scenery for school plays two years running.

INTERESTS AND HOBBIES

I enjoy sport and play in the college's football team. I enjoy popular music and going to the cinema with friends.

REFERENCES

Ms Jean Willers
Principal
Wellesbourne Community College
Burns Road
Wellesbourne
SA33 3RR
01889 299384

Dawn Collins
Manager
Speedy Pizza
High Street
Wellesbourne
SA33 5TY
01294 494837

Example of a CV for a school leaver – 3

MAYA SINGH
16 Wilberforce Road
Manchester
M14 6BD
0161 234 5678

DOB 16 May 1985   Nationality: British

SKILLS PROFILE

Communicating and Team Working

- Effective written and verbal communication skills

- Enjoy working as part of a team – our group project in Business Studies got the highest grade of the year

Commercial Awareness

- Business Studies A level (B) – for other qualifications see 'Education and Qualifications'

- Bi-lingual English/Bengali

Personal Drive

- Self starter

- Always meet deadlines

Technical Skills

- Competent Word user

- Internet proficient

- Some knowledge of databases

Language Proficiency

English and Bengali	Fluent
French and German	To GCSE standard

EMPLOYMENT HISTORY

Jan 2004 – Jun 2004   Griggs Insurance, Saturday Receptionist, High Street, Salford, Manchester M14 8RW

Reception duties including answering telephone, filing, greeting customers

Dec 2002-Jun 2003   The Corner Shop, Wilberforce Road, Salford, Manchester M14 6BD

Paper round, delivering papers correctly.

EDUCATION AND QUALIFICATIONS

2002-2004   Mill Road 6th Form College, Salford, Manchester M14 5TT

A level: English (B), Business Studies (B), French (A)

1996 – 2002   Maple Community College, Maple Road, Salford, Manchester M14 3DE

7 GCSEs including: Maths (B) Geography (A) Religious Studies (B) German (D)

INTERESTS

I am a member of the college girl's football team. I also enjoy reading, cooking and learning languages.

Example of a CV for a school leaver – 4

Jane Collinson
22 Corfield Road
Swansea
SA3 7RG
01792 554467
dob 16.5.87
jane.collinson@nntn.net

Personal Profile

Recent school leaver with excellent administrative and wordprocessing skills. I am a fast learner, flexible and enjoy working as part of a team.

Skills

- NVQ level 2 Customer Service

- Excellent written and verbal communication skills

- Good decision making skills

- Able to work on own initiative

- Typing at 35 wpm

- Some knowledge of Excel

EMPLOYMENT HISTORY

Feb 2003   Harper Building Society, High Street, Llandor, Swansea SA9 3LK.

During my two weeks work experience with this building society I was involved in:

- opening and distributing the post

- filing

- operating the switchboard

- sending information out to customers

- typing.

Jan-Nov 2002   Rebecca's Greengrocery, 247 Maldon Road, Swansea SA1 3PS.

Saturday assistant. Whilst working at Rebecca's my tasks included:

- unloading produce vans

- arranging produce attractively

- checking quality of produce

- serving customers

- cash handling.

EDUCATION AND QUALIFICATIONS

2003   Llandor Comprehensive School, Swanns Road, Llandor, Swansea SA9 6CV.

Seven GCSEs including:
Maths grade C   English grade A   Business studies grade B
NVQ 2 Customer service

INTEREST AND HOBBIES

I have many interests including embroidery, reading, socialising with friends and swimming.

REFERENCES

Mr T Thomas   Katherine Calvin
Harper Building Society   Llandor Comprehensive School
High Street   Swanns Road
Llandor   Llandor
Swansea   Swansea
SA9 3LK   SA9 6CV
01729 883210   01729 453234

CV for a college leaver

James Robinson
231 Upper High Street
Cambridge
CB4 5LF
01223 554633
james@robinson.com

PROFESSIONAL PROFILE

A hardworking graduate with a keen interest in, and commitment to, social issues. My interests have given me invaluable experience in the field of research and dealing with people and difficult situations.

QUALIFICATIONS

Anglia Polytechnic University, East Road, Cambridge CB1 2ER.

2000-2003	BA Social Sciences 2:1
	My course included economics, politics, sociology, philosophy, geography and statistics. My thesis was in deprivation within inner cities in Britain. I was awarded the Williams prize for best thesis of the year.
2000	A level English (B), Sociology (A)

CAREER TO DATE

April 2003 – present	Bath Inner City Survey, Grosvenor Road, Bath BA1 1ET
Researcher	This temporary post has given me good experience of:

- qualitative research methods
- methodical working
- business environment
- working as part of a team.

Sept 2000 – Apr 2003	B & Y DIY Store, Huntingdon Road, Cambridge, CB4 3BN

Weekend Clerical Assistant – this part-time post offered me considerable experience in:

- office routine
- handling difficult situations
- customer service.

INTERESTS

I am keen on keeping fit and as well as playing several sports, I teach a circuit class once a week. I also enjoy travel and spending time with friends.

ADDITIONAL INFORMATION

I have a full clean driving licence. I was, for two years, involved with stage design for a local amateur dramatics society whilst at college. I have good keyboard skills and can design a simple web page.

REFERENCES

Mr T Edwards	Ms K Lee
Bath Inner City Survey	27 Declan Street
Grosvenor Road	Cambridge
Bath	CB3 2QW
BA2 1ET	01223 434909

CV for application for position as nanny

YASMIN COLEMAN

CACHE Level 3 Diploma
in Child Care and Education (DCE)
Full Clean Driving Licence
DOB 24.1.86

3 Robbins Way
Brighton
BR4 3MN
01832 887451

SKILLS

An enthusiastic and committed newly-qualified nursery nurse with previous childcare experience. I hold first aid and food hygiene certificates. My particular strengths are:

- real interest in child development
- patience
- honouring parent's chosen childcare style
- flexibility

CHILD CARE TRAINING

CACHE level 3 Diploma in Child Care and Education

Brighton Regional College 2002-2004

My group project was on psychological development of children between the ages of one and three.

Education

Brighton Community College.
1997- 2002

6 GCSEs including Maths, English, Child Development

WORK EXPERIENCE

Saturday Nanny · **Mr & Mrs Bell Sept 03 – May 04**

I worked Saturdays for Mrs Bell looking after her two children aged 3 months and 2 years.

Classroom Assistant · **Mr J Wibberley Sept 02 – May 03**

College placement assisting in classrooms with children aged 4-6

Nursery Assistant · **Mrs J Ross Oct 03 – June 04**

College placement assisting with nursery children aged 6 months to 2 years.

OTHER EXPERIENCE

I have two younger brothers and a younger sister whom I often take care of. I also regularly babysit for local families.

HOBBIES AND INTERESTS

I am interested in arts and crafts and enjoy swimming and aerobics. I read, go dancing with friends and enjoy needlework.

REFERENCES

Mr & Mrs Bell	Mr J Wibberley	Mrs J Ross
27 Pargeter Green	James Primary School	The Nursery
Hove	Sheila Road	Sydney Street
BR1 2WW	Brighton	Brighton
01832 332242	BN 3 4TT	BN6 6KU
	01832 564739	01832 439081

Chapter ten
Job application forms

You should read this chapter:

- before you begin to work on a job application form.

By the end of this chapter you should know:

- how to use your self analysis

- how to present information about yourself

- how to use job descriptions and person specifications to shape your answers

- how to use evidence of success.

I advertised for an Aviation Bird Controller. The job is to try to keep birds away from flightpaths at airports by manipulating the environment and other non-violent methods. In response to the question 'Why do you think you're suited to this job?' one person wrote 'I like kill all things, pidjins and vermin.' Awful! This guy was not very literate and had obviously shown his application form to a friend who was not much better. The friend had used a different colour pen and added some of his own comments in very distinctively different handwriting (which was almost as bad as the applicant's).

Quote from an aviation bird control manager

Guess who didn't even get an interview?

The quote above just had to go at the beginning of the chapter because it's such an extreme (and true) example of what not to write. Hopefully, you're not applying for jobs to 'kill all things', but by working through this chapter you can ensure that your application form avoids errors of any sort.

There are several advantages to completing application forms. The format is prepared for you, you simply have to fill in the spaces and sometimes the space provided suggests how much you should write. The form also tells you what information to provide, as well as the format and this saves you having to make decisions about these issues.

Some disadvantages are that you may have little flexibility to express yourself. Also it is difficult to complete an application form using a wordprocessor, although now many organisations have their forms on the web and you can often send it electronically. Even if you can't, you can often fill it in on your screen, print it off and then post it. Some organisations use the same form for applicants for all their jobs and so it may be difficult to provide the information you want to get across. Almost all forms have the dreaded 'Tell me why you want the job' box – usually the biggest box. Luckily this page is dead easy to complete when you know the trick.

Almost all forms ask first the familiar questions about name, address, etc. Some organisations that are committed to equal opportunities may not ask for your first name, simply an initial. This is to avoid gender bias.

But let's go back a step. If you have read Chapters two, three and four you will already have collected a mass of relevant information about yourself which you can use on an application form. If you have not read these chapters yet, do go back and do so. They include a range of activities to help you to analyse yourself and your skills and to work out the best way to sell yourself.

For each job you are interested in, you will need to go through this process again, albeit in less detail. Your aim will be to match what you say about yourself to the job description and person specification supplied to you as well as to anything you know about the organisation. Remember, even if you are not supplied with a job description or person specification you can make a fair job of working out what they would be (refer back to Chapter two if you're not sure).

Let me re-cap on some of the major points from those chapters:

- you need to identify your skills and experience relevant to the job you are applying for

- you need to display your education and training to best effect

- you need to write about your leisure activities in a way that shows you to be a good all round person with some relevant interests

- you should be able to write about yourself using a range of 'positive' words

- you should have identified those things about yourself which make you stand out from the crowd.

Additionally, and specifically for each job you are applying for, work out what you can offer the job and the organisation, why you want the job, and why you're applying for this type of job *now*. This type of thinking preparation helps you not just at the application stage but also during the interview should you be offered one.

As you plan how to complete your application form keep these points in mind and try to get inside the reader's head. Try to work out what they are looking for and how you can show that you have it (or at least some of it).

With this preparation in mind you are almost ready to start on the form. But two things first. Photocopy it. No smudges, coffee stains or scribbles allowed. *Then read the instructions on the form twice.*

> *'We ask for people to complete the application form in their own handwriting (that is emphasised on the form) and I feel really irritated when people type it or write in block letters. The job involves some log keeping and I have to read the logs – I hate having to struggle to read bad handwriting.'*

> ### Quote from a manager

Most forms are very straightforward and many now make a point of asking questions in very simple language. Nevertheless, the number of forms received with crossings out is amazing.

The dreaded 'blank page' (or 'Further information')

Probably the section most dreaded in application forms is the one that is pretty much blank. It is usually headed 'Further information in support of your application' or 'How you meet the selection criteria' or similar. Most forms give you no guidance on how to complete this section.

Luckily, there are tips that can make this process really straightforward. Follow these simple steps:

1. Check if the form, or guidance notes on how to complete it if provided, tell you what the selection criteria are. They are almost always the job description, person specification or both. If you are not told, assume it is both.

2. At the top of the blank page write a general introduction. Something like 'In support of my application I will provide examples of my experience in the same order as shown in the job description and person specification'. Before that you could also include the professional profile as described in Chapter eight – *Dazzling CVs*.

3. Study the job description and person specification.

4. For each item on the job description and person specification write something about your experience of that item. You can even number your paragraphs in the same way as on the job description and person specification.

Example

Job Description/ Person Spec. Item	Example you might give
Type manager's letters	During my work placement I was responsible for all the typing for two managers for a period of three weeks. My typing speed is currently 40wpm.
Filing	Whilst in my work placement I was shown the filing system and accurately filed all my own documents.
Customer service skills	I dealt with customers every Saturday for two years whilst working in a shoe shop. I received on-the-job training in customer service and became quite skilled at helping customers find shoes they wanted.
Able to work alone	I am a well-motivated person, able to work alone. For example, I always hand in course work on time.
Able to work as part of a team	Some of my course was groupwork. I enjoyed working as part of a team and found myself taking an active part in all discussions. We achieved a grade A for our last project.

Easy!

So few candidates understand how to do this that you'll be streets ahead if you follow these simple steps.

Example application form

 Cambridgeshire County Council

Confidential   *Making equality a reality*

A P P L I C A T I O N   F O R M

Please read the guidance notes before completing this form.

■ JOB DETAILS

Application for	
Directorate	Reference No.

■ PERSONAL DETAILS

Surname	Initials
Address for correspondence	
Tel. No. (Home)	Mobile/Work Tel No

■ EDUCATION (from age 11)

School/College/University attended	Certificates/Qualifications obtained	Dates from and to (month/year)

Membership of professional bodies or other relevant qualifications

Details of relevant training courses   month/year

■ PRESENT OR MOST RECENT EMPLOYMENT (including unpaid activities)

Name of Employer

Address

Post Held

month/year

Date started

Notice required
if applicable

Current Salary

Present Employment ☐   Recent Employment ☐   (Please Indicate)

Main Duties and Responsibilities

■ PREVIOUS EMPLOYMENT (continue on a separate sheet if necessary)

Have you previously worked for Cambridgeshire County Council?   Yes ☐   No ☐

If yes, please include below with details of all previous employment:

Employer's name and address	Post held	Dates from & to Month/Year	Reason for Leaving

■ HOW YOU MEET THE SELECTION CRITERIA
(read guidance notes before completing)

■ REFEREES

Name

Address
Including
E-mail

Tel. No.

Occupation or Relationship to you

May we contact your referee prior to interview if shortlisted?   Yes [ ] No [ ]

Name

Address
Including
E-mail

Tel. No.

Occupation or Relationship to you

Yes [ ] No [ ]

■ REHABILITATION OF OFFENDERS ACT

Have you been convicted, cautioned or court martialled for any relevant criminal offence?   Yes [ ] No [ ]

Is there any relevant court action pending against you?   Yes [ ] No [ ]

■ DECLARATION

I confirm that the information I have given on this form is correct and complete and that misleading statements may be sufficient for cancelling any agreements made. I understand that, in the event of being shortlisted for interview, I will be required to complete a confidential declaration in respect of my health. *Because of the sensitive nature of the duties that the postholder may sometimes be expected to undertake, I also understand that a "Declaration of Criminal Record" form may have to be completed.** This will include details of any criminal convictions, cautions, reprimands and final warnings and any other information that may have a bearing on my suitability for the post.

*The part in italics only applies to posts requiring a Standard or Enhanced Level of Disclosure.

Are you related to, or do you have a close personal relationship with, any Councillor or employee of Cambridgeshire County Council.   Yes [ ] No [ ]

If yes, please state their name and position

I declare that all the above information is correct.

Signature   Date

Return the completed form to: Recruitment Team, Cambridgeshire County Council, Box ELH 1403, Shire Hall, Castle Hill, Cambridge, CB3 0AP.
E-mail to recruitment@cambridgeshire.gov.uk

By using the real application form on pages 151-154, we'll look at how to present all this information about yourself as effectively as possible. Although advice is focused on this form, the points would apply to other forms you may have to complete.

Do read the forms very carefully and follow instructions *exactly*; your application may be rejected out of hand if you don't. And remember to work on a photocopy of the form until you're happy you've got it exactly right. When you've completed it, keep a copy for reference for when you get invited to interview.

Although the form you receive when you apply for a job may not be exactly the same as this one, it is likely to have much in common.

Applicants who are using this form, from Cambridgeshire County Council, are also given written advice on how to complete the form. If you are offered advice *always follow it precisely*. You will see that you can complete the form and send it in online. However, if you fill it in by hand you must use *black* ink (this is so it can be easily photocopied).

Whilst most of the sections will be easy for you to complete, you must take special care with the section 'How you meet the selection criteria'. The advice given along with the form tells you that the essential criteria against which your application will be judged is the person specification, so you would need to study that document carefully. These advice guidelines give a series of questions to consider:

■ How do your abilities and experience make you suitable for the post?

■ Why are you applying for this post?

■ If the job requires mobility, can you drive, do you have a clean licence and do you have use of a car or other motor vehicle?

■ What are your interests outside work?

If you follow the advice already given in this chapter under the section headed 'The dreaded blank page' you will find this section fairly easy to complete. Remember that when answering the question 'Why are you applying for this post?' the employer does not expect answers such as 'It's on my bus route', or 'The pay is good'. They want to hear why you want to work for THEM and what you can offer THEM. So your answers should include something along the lines of 'I am interested in working for your organisation because it has a good reputation for staff development and excellent service. I am particularly interested in this post because it would allow me to use my existing skills and develop further skills.' Remember, they look at things mostly from their point of view, not yours.

Many application forms do not ask you so specifically about periods of employment, unemployment etc. If the form does not ask this you can 'disguise' short periods of unemployment or jobs you didn't stay in long by 'losing' them between dates. For example, if you were unemployed between May and August 2003, you simply don't put the months on the application form. However, to do this when you are so specifically asked to state periods of unemployment etc would effectively constitute a lie and could lead to dismissal if you were offered the job. For this reason, I would not recommend 'losing' any periods of unemployment on a form like this – own up.

When it comes to 'Reason for Leaving' you may need to use tact. There are a few unwritten golden rules about explaining why you left a job. Here they are.

■ Always try to make the reason for leaving sound positive rather than negative. Something to wanted to go to, rather than something you wanted to get away from.

■ Try to avoid saying you were sacked if you can, but don't tell a lie.

■ Don't say something like, 'Because I didn't get on with the boss' – the reader will not know this person and may wonder if *you* are a trouble-maker.

■ Employers like to see that people have moved on for logical reasons – for promotion, to widen skills and experience, because you have moved from one part of the country to another, to return to education.

■ Mentioning redundancy can be OK, although sometimes employers may wonder why you were chosen to be made redundant. If this was because the company or department was closed down then say so, rather than simply 'made redundant'.

For qualifications present your information in a consistent and easy to read manner. This means not mixing, for example, 3 August 2004 with

3.8.04. If any of your qualifications are unusual or were obtained abroad you may want to add an explanatory note so that the shortlister can make comparisons with other qualifications.

Declaration

Simply your signature and the date. If you send in your form electronically, you will be asked to sign it when you attend for interview. Remember that all application forms should be accompanied by a covering letter, however brief. Chapter eleven covers this in further detail.

Equal opportunities forms

Some application forms also have an equal opportunities section. Often this is a separate sheet or one that is torn off the main application form. Organisations use this information to check whether they are discriminating against any groups. In many organisations this information is detached from the form before the shortlister sees it.

Other possible sections

One large employer on their application form asks for your experience of working in a group. Ideally, they want a work group but say they will accept school/college experience. Some examples of group work and what they are trying to achieve would be:

Group	Achievement
Group project work at school, college or work	'Completed project on local history meeting deadline. Our group achieved a grade 'A.'
Fund-raising activities	'Raised £1,250 with fun run for SCOPE.'
Working in a team	'We worked well together for the local history project, each taking a separate section but meeting regularly and helping each other as necessary.'
Planning a party with others	'Our class committee arranged a very successful end of year party.'
Member of the football club committee	'We ensure that health and safety regulations are always adhered to.'

If you are then asked what you enjoyed about working with other people in the group, be honest – there will be things you enjoyed. Common answers might include learning from each other, helping each other to be creative, working towards a goal, socialising with other people, learning new skills, and having a sense of comradeship.

If you are asked what you did not enjoy about working with a group again, be honest. Groups are great, they can achieve so much more than individuals working alone. But they can also be frustrating. Common problems you may have noticed are:

■ some people saying too much

■ others saying too little

■ some people doing a lot of work

■ others doing very little

■ some people being late and/or unreliable

■ people having impractical ideas

■ people getting off the point.

And what did you learn about yourself and how you work with other people? Did you learn that you were:

■ creative	■ patient
■ impatient	■ hard-working
■ always late	■ a natural leader
■ good at fine detail	■ good at cheering people up
■ good at finding out information	■ happiest sticking to the rules
■ thoughtful towards others	■ jokey
■ challenging	■ argumentative.

These are all things a prospective employer would be interested to know. Select carefully those items to include, remember to consider what is needed in the job. By the way, if you realise that you have some negative points here – perhaps you are impatient or always late, do work to rectify this. Problems such as this will hold back your career.

'One applicant wrote "I have a good sense of humour – I'm from Liverpool!". It made us smile too, although it didn't necessarily impress us as we are not from Liverpool and wondered if it meant that the writer felt that only Liverpudlians have a sense of humour.'

Quote from manager of a small firm

Application form from a small organisation

Having looked at the application form for a large organisation, let's look at one from a company employing eight people. The company specialises in moving specialised freight within both the UK and abroad.

Before we look at it, you might like to see the list of questions the managers ask themselves when interviewing candidates. It shows what they are looking for, even at the application stage, and reminds you of the need to always try to get inside the interviewer's head.

Some of these questions may seem unusual. The form is very specifically designed to ensure that they appoint someone who will fit in with the existing work group – the company is run on very democratic lines. The same form is used for all vacancies. This particular company employs young people (no one over 40), mostly males. They are expected to work hard and put in long hours. There is a lot of overlap between each other's work, and people will generally 'muck in' and have a go at anything when necessary. There is a lot of humour in the workplace. There is also a high commitment to getting it right, looking after the customer and developing the business.

If you live locally to the company you are applying to, you may be able to find out some of these details if not all. You can find out by word of mouth, information you can gather when phoning the organisation for an application form, asking your Connexions/careers service or the Jobcentre/Jobcentre Plus office, local or national press, your library or the internet.

Obviously no employer is going to give you such a list normally, but you may be able to work out for yourself what their list might be, based on the job description and person specification. For more details, see *Excel at Interviews*, also by Patricia McBride, published by Lifetime Careers Publishing.

Interview Checklist

Applicant's name ....

Question	Yes	No	Comments
Is the person outgoing?			
Is this person shy?			
Is this person ambitious?			
Has this person shown ambition in the past?			
Would this person drive the van and do packing?			
Could this person fit in well with the rest of the team?			
Could this person organise others?			
Does this person seem organised?			
Would this person work long hours?			
Could this person use the computer?			
Will this person understand freight?			
Can this person communicate?			
Is this person over-sensitive?			
Has this person got a sense of humour?			

This company actually uses two application forms – applicants have to complete both. The first asks for factual details of name, schools attended, qualifications, etc. Remember when completing factual information to keep the job description and person specification in mind at all times.

> *I'm very wary of people who are too obvious when they complete an application form. If they use too many of the words we've used, I think 'Oh, he's just read the job description and chucked in a few words'.*

Quote from a manager at the freight company

As we have already studied these areas using the typical application form, we'll look at the freight company's second form here.

But before we start you need to know a little about the job itself. There is no person specification although one would be easy to work out from the interview checklist opposite.

AIRFREIGHT OPERATIONS ASSISTANT

JOB DESCRIPTION

1. Deal with customer orders.
2. Establish how customer requirements can be best met.
3. Identify how to ship goods to their destination.
4. Use computer to record all stages of the customer contract.
5. Drive the van when necessary.
6. Load and unload goods when required.
7. Undertake any other tasks as identified by the management.

APPLICATION FOR EMPLOYMENT

AIRFREIGHT OPERATIONS ASSISTANT

In order to assist in the selection process we require you to complete both types of application form. The first is a standard format which provides basic information. This second form is designed to find out more in depth information about your past work experience and personality. The greater information that you supply the better the selection process will be. This form completed as honestly and comprehensively as possible will lead to a more satisfactory outcome for **you** and the company.

1. Which periods of your life were the ones you consider your happiest? Explain why:

2. Please describe situations in your past experience which were the most fulfilling. Explain why:

3. What work situations have been the most difficult to deal with? Explain why they were difficult and what you did to overcome them:

4. What kind of job are you looking for? Explain why:

5. When do you feel most under pressure in or out of work?

6. What are your aims and aspirations? What practical steps are you taking to achieve them?

Signed:

Dated:

All information submitted by applicants will be treated in strict confidence. This information will not be released to unauthorised persons both in or out of the company.

You will see that in the introductory paragraph you are told that the organisation is trying to find out about your past work experience and personality. Their aim is to try to get people to be honest about themselves and their experiences and where possible to get people to drop their application if they feel it is not appropriate. This is an important point that many organisations overlook. If the advertisement is not tailored very tightly to the job and to identifying what the organisation requires of the person, they can find themselves inundated with unsuitable applicants. This is a waste of time for everyone.

You have been able to sell your skills and talents in the most effective way in the first application form from this company. Now you should work on selling your personality.

It seems to me that questions of this nature are trying to find out about something mentioned elsewhere in this book – emotional intelligence. Employers are often faced with several candidates who have the skills and experience to do the job, but have to ask themselves how well these people operate on a people level also. Just a reminder that Daniel Goleman in *'Working with Emotional Intelligence'* (published by Bloomsbury, 1999) refers to people who are emotionally intelligent as having:

Self-awareness – recognising your own feelings, knowing your strengths and weaknesses and being self confident

Self-regulation – self control, being trustworthy and conscientious, being flexible and innovative

Motivation – wanting to achieve the best, being a self-starter and being optimistic

Empathy – understanding how other people think and feel, anticipating the needs of others, being politically aware (that is knowing how their organisation works)

Socially skilled – being a good communicator, managing conflict well, being able to work as part of a team.

So do bear in mind the need to demonstrate these qualities when answering questions of this type.

1. **Which periods of your life were the ones you consider your happiest? Explain why.**

Gosh, this is difficult to answer. Everyone will have a different happiest time, but here are some ideas to prompt you:

- holidays

- meeting a new girl/boyfriend

- family gatherings

- a particular year at school or college

- helping in a voluntary capacity.

Remember to say why. Was the holiday happy because you had an opportunity to travel with friends around Europe doing your own thing? Be honest in your answer, but keep the details of the job in mind.

2. **Please describe situations in your past experience that were the most fulfilling. Explain why.**

This appears to be a very similar question to the first one. There is no 'right' way to answer this or any of the other questions. One suggestion here might be to answer the first question with a personal experience and this question with a work experience. You could even mention that this is how you propose to tackle the questions. Some examples of fulfilling work experience would be:

- feeling you've done a job really well

- setting up a new system

- seeing a project through to the end

- helping other people in some way.

3. **What work situations have been the most difficult to deal with?**

Explain why they were difficult and what you did to overcome them.

This sort of question can be tricky if you are just beginning your career, but even at 16 or 21 or whatever we have all faced difficult situations. At the very least you could write about how it felt to settle into your work placement, meeting new people, learning the routines, etc.

'My work placement was in a very busy sales office. The manager was away for my first day, so I felt at a loss. I coped with this by…'

'I worked in a home for elderly people and one of the residents, to whom I'd become very attached, had a heart attack when I was in her room. I…'

'My industrial placement was as a receptionist in a hotel. One of the clients tried to pay by credit card, but the credit card company refused to clear the payment. The customer became very abusive and aggressive as a result. I responded by…'

'I changed schools half way through my second year of GCSE and the syllabus was different because of a different examining board. I caught up by…'

'One of my college lecturers explained important topics in a really confusing way. As a result I had to…'

Some tips here. Don't write as if it's all doom and gloom, don't complain about other people, and don't run down the organisation. Remember emotional intelligence. Take responsibility for your own difficulties and finding a way through them. This doesn't mean making yourself sound incompetent, none of us is perfect. Do say very positively how you overcome the problems:

'I quickly realised that I could settle into the job better if I understood how the other departments worked. I asked another manager if I could visit other departments and she agreed to this. I found it very helpful and it gave me a face to put to names I would later speak to on the phone.'

'I called for help and loosened the lady's clothing. I stayed with her until the ambulance arrived.'

'I kept calm and suggested that the angry customer speak to the manager. I showed him into the office and tried to make him feel more comfortable.'

'It was very difficult at the engineering company because everyone was so demoralised. However, it seemed to help when I let them know that I felt I could learn a lot from them. I learnt a lot about the way in which businesses operate, too.'

4. What kind of job are you looking for? Explain why.

Well, obviously you are looking for the job being advertised or you wouldn't be applying. However, this question really wants a more complete answer. Are you looking for a job that offers:

- excitement

- challenge

- routine

- variety

- good company

- good financial rewards

- valuable experience.

Whichever answer you give (and yours may be different from the above) expand a bit so that the reader gets a real flavour of what you are like as a person.

5. When do you feel most under pressure in or out of work?

Mmm, this is one to be careful with because you could really damage your chances of an interview. Keep in mind the organisation. For this company, it wouldn't be wise to say that you felt under pressure when you were too busy, or had to work late or didn't have a fixed routine. In fact there are not many jobs where it would be wise to admit to these problems. You could consider mentioning pressures like:

- being unable to finish the work as well as you'd like

- being unable to use creativity and initiative

- being unchallenged by your work or responsibilities

- having to do repetitive work

- not really feeling involved as part of a team.

6. What are your aims and aspirations? What practical steps are you taking to achieve them?

Do you know what your aims and aspirations are? Have you a career plan in your head or on paper somewhere? There is a lot of research that shows that people who have a career plan not only get where they want to go, they get there faster than they expect. In fact, they get there faster than their college friends who maybe did better in their exams. Having a plan is tremendously helpful. And this is a fairly typical interview question if not one often asked on application forms. For that reason, you should spend some time working through where you see yourself in five or ten years, or by the time you retire.

'Safe' aims and aspirations would include working in a job you enjoy, developing your skills, climbing a career ladder and learning about the industry in question.

Have you taken any practical steps? Has the pattern of your education and career to date been logical and focused, or are you still trying to find your niche? Practical steps you may have taken include:

- taking the right courses

- talking to a careers counsellor

- studying hard

- developing relevant skills either through work or in some other way

- finding relevant jobs, even if part-time or vacation work

- learning transferable skills from jobs that were not exactly what you wanted

- learning to use your initiative

- keeping up to date with what's going on in your work field.

No application form is easy or quick to complete – after all, it's an important document. A more complex one like this will probably take you several attempts. Look at it in a positive light – if you are offered an interview (and your chances will be greatly increased if you spend the time now), you will have done much of the preparation work for the interview. For information on how to handle interviews, see *Excel at Interviews*, also by Patricia McBride from Lifetime Careers Publishing.

Chapter checklist

When completing your application form, have you:

- taken at least one photocopy before you start? Work on that copy until you are sure you have it exactly right.

- read the instructions on the form carefully and followed them to the letter?

- read the job description, person specification and any information you have about the company thoroughly?

- tried to work out exactly what type of person the organisation is looking for by studying their selection criteria?

- analysed your skills, experience and personality highlighting those that fit in with the needs of the job you're applying for?

- been consistent with the way you present material? Make it easy for the reader to shortlist you.

- left the form after the first draft so that you have an opportunity to re-think what you've written?

- polished the form until you are completely happy that it gets across exactly the message you want?

- made a good copy with no mistakes?

- kept a copy for future reference?

- remembered your covering letter?

Chapter eleven
The covering letter

You should read this chapter:

■ when you have completed your CV or application form.

By the end of this chapter you should know:

■ what points to consider when writing a covering letter

■ who to address the letter to

■ how to write letters when applying for a specific job.

The importance of covering letters

Your covering letter can be important as your CV, yet they are often poorly written or overlooked altogether.

The covering letter is an opportunity to further sell yourself as a person, as well as to highlight any major points you think will impress. It is a quick introduction to you and your skillset and as such saves the shortlister time and effort.

Making a start

By the time you get to reading this chapter you have probably spent some time preparing your CV or completing your application form and you're probably thinking, 'I can't think of another word to say!' Actually, it's easy from here.

If you are sending a CV, you may have chosen to leave out some of the 'additional information' at the end of your CV to form the meat of your covering letter. If you've completed an application form, the odds are that the layout of the form didn't give you much opportunity to say everything you want to say.

But let's do the easy bit first. Whether you are writing in response to a particular job advert or speculatively you must get the letter to the correct person. This may be obvious if the name was stated in the advertisement or was with the information sent to you by the organisation. However, if it wasn't or if you are writing speculatively, spend the time and effort to find out who the correct person is. It's a small point, but it does show the reader that you are able to use your initiative. You simply have to phone the organisation and ask the switchboard who would be the correct person.

Be prepared though. Often switchboard operators don't listen well and before you know where you are they've put you through to the personnel manager (or whoever) without having given you their name or having been requested to do so. So instead of a nice informal chat to the operator, you're speaking instantly to the decision maker. If that leaves you saying 'Um, um' a few times, you won't make a good impression. So prepare beforehand what you want to say if this happens. If you are inexperienced at speaking to people 'in authority' make a few notes of what you want to say and have these in front of you. These include what job you are interested in – also noting where you found out about the job and any job reference number, some basic facts about yourself that relate to the job and why you are interested in the job.

> *'I admire people for going for jobs a little above their present experience level. However, people must have the absolute basics. I advertised for a job recently where it was stated that the postholder would need excellent oral and written skills. Someone wrote in their covering letter, 'I am not very good at expressing myself on paper due to a poor education'.'*

> *Quote from a manager*

Practical issues

Your covering letter should be on good quality A4 writing paper, preferably the same as your CV if you've sent one or unlined writing paper. DON'T use lined A4 paper with holes punched down the side, pretty paper Aunt Mary sent you last Christmas or anything else. IT WON'T IMPRESS and you'll simply look unprofessional.

Layout for letters is usually aligned left, that means:

- no indents

- everything lined up to the left but 'ragged' on the right.

Also:

- punctuation marks are not used after the address.

- the date is written in full but without 'th' 'rd' etc

- the main heading is highlighted in some way, usually with bold type. If you are handwriting the letter (and some employers ask you to do this), the heading can be written in capitals or underlined

- use 'Yours sincerely' if you write to the person by name. If you really can't find out the person's name and have to write anonymously, it's 'Dear Sir or Madam', and 'Yours faithfully' – note that 'sincerely' and 'faithfully' do not start with capital letters

- write Enc. at the bottom of your letter to show that you have enclosed something (your CV, application form or anything else)

- remember to include your telephone number in the letter somewhere, either under your address or in the body of the letter. Include an email address too if you have one. I know this information will be on the CV or application form but make it easy for them to phone you.

Here is what I mean:

Your address
etc
etc
etc
postcode
telephone number
email address

Bloggs Engineering Works
Unit 7
St Martins Industrial Estate
Bloxburg
Avon
BB22 3EE

Date

Dear Ms Stedman

Vacancy for Trainee Engineer

Opening comments.

Body of your letter, may take one or more paragraphs.

Final sentence.

Yours sincerely

Your name (printed clearly under your signature)
Enc.

Occasionally you will be asked to write the covering letter by hand. Generally this means that they want to check your handwriting either because they want to ensure that it is legible, because this is necessary for the job, or they plan to get a graphologist to check it to make an assessment of your personality. Graphology isn't used terribly widely so it's more likely to be the first reason. Obviously this means that you need to use your 'best' handwriting.

Whether your letter is handwritten, typed or wordprocessed make sure that you write good grammer (better than this, that is...). If you are unsure, ask someone you trust to check it.

Content

Your covering letter should sound confident and lively. It should tell the reader in very brief terms (using bullet points or not – the choice is yours) why you'd be good for the job. Don't overdo it and look pushy or big-headed, but simply let them know what you can do. This means that you have to summarise in no more than about four or five sentences what you've said in the CV or application form. You may choose to add some new information, perhaps the fact that you'd like to move to that area or when you are available for interview. Remember to use all those positive sounding words again.

A good general format is:

■ **Paragraph 1** – brief introduction to yourself including a description of the job you are applying for or your 'career objective'. Give details of why you want this particular job with this particular organisation. Sound enthusiastic. Show you've done your research.

■ **Paragraphs 2/3** – a short description of your education, skills and any other information you think they should know. Remember to target everything you write to the vacancy you are applying for. Remember also to use key words to attract the attention of the human or software package reading your letter. If necessary, mention any negative points in your application if you can explain them away – for example poor exam results because of illness.

■ **Paragraph 3** – a closing paragraph mentioning contact details (other than those in your address at the top of the page).

On the next few pages are some advertisements and the covering letter to go with each one.

Assistant Secretary

Hawkins Ltd requires an assistant secretary to provide secretarial and administrative support. The duties are varied and will include typing (copy and audio), arranging meetings and taking minutes.

Applicants should have a good standard of education, preferably with GCSE English and OCR Level 2 Certificate in Text Processing or similar. They should have excellent communications skills and be able to wordprocess.

Applications in writing, including full CV and details of two referees, should be sent to:

Ms. M. Ahmed
Personnel Manager
Hawkins Ltd
Peterson Road
Oxford
OX1 2DD

Dear Mrs Ahmed

Vacancy for Assistant Secretary

Please find enclosed my CV in application for the above vacancy which was advertised in this week's 'Oxford Reporter'[1] As you will see I am just about to leave the Regional College having completed a Pitmans Administration & Secretarial Procedures level 3 course. Part of the course was a work placement where I was given valuable experience in all the areas outlined in your letter[2]

I am particularly interested in working for Hawkins as I know several people who work for the company and believe it to be an excellent company to work for[3].

I am a hard working person, able to work unsupervised once I 'know the ropes' although I also enjoy working as part of a team[4]. My communication skills are good – I have been Chairperson of the Students' Association for the past eighteen months[5].

I look forward to hearing from you[6]. I am available for interview after the 22nd or earlier by arrangement[7].

This is a pretty good letter, bouncy and confident.

1. The applicant has remembered to mention where s/he saw the job advertised.

2. The applicant could have enlarged on this a little, perhaps repeating the tasks as outlined in the advertisement for emphasis.

3. No harm in a bit of flattery, don't overdo it though!

4. This sentence highlights personal strengths all employers would value.

5. Although this information would probably be the CV it's worth repeating here to emphasise the point.

6. Sounds confident without being pushy.

7. This sounds as if you have other things going on in your life. To simply say *'I'm available any time'* sounds as if you have no calls on your time at all (this may be true but you don't say so).

Direct Marketing Assistant

Griffin Ltd are looking for a well motivated and enthusiastic person to join their small marketing department.

The person appointed will be part of a team responsible for the direct marketing promotion of the company.

We are looking for someone with an interest in learning how to:

- copywrite and proofread
- analyse campaign data
- liaise with other departments and printers.

You should be a good communicator both verbally and in writing. Keyboard skills are an advantage.

Please send your CV and covering letter to:

John Farnsworth
Griffin Ltd
27 Dallow Road
York

Dear Mr Farnsworth

Direct Marketing Assistant

Please find enclosed my CV in application for the above job advertised in this week's *Recorder*.

I have recently left Colmsford Regional College where I successfully completed a BTEC in Business Studies[1]. I particularly enjoyed the module on marketing[2] and went on to do a six-week placement with Briggs Hardware in their Marketing Department[3].

[4]While at Briggs, I learnt to use wordprocessing and desktop publishing packages[5]. Last year I was deputy editor of the student magazine and these skills were fully tested there![6]

I would love[7] to work in Direct Marketing, especially at Griffins as I feel it is an exciting field at the moment[8].

Yours sincerely,

Well, as an employer I'd be reaching for the phone to see this person...

1. Two selling points in one sentence. S/he has 'successfully' completed the course (positive word) and mentioned a very relevant course, too.

2. Likewise, 'enjoyed' and mentioned the most relevant module.

3. This placement must have offered a lot of valuable skills, pity they weren't mentioned in a little more detail.

4. The writer has managed to resist the temptation of starting two consecutive paragraphs with 'I'.

5. This is a higher level of computer literacy than many college leavers and is certainly worth highlighting.

6. A little humour doesn't hurt, and this is connected directly to really useful experience editing a magazine.

7. Is this a bit gushing? Perhaps, but it comes across and sincere and enthusiastic.

TRAINEE WINDSCREEN FITTER

Screensafe plc are looking for a trainee to join their team of windscreen fitters. Body shop experience would be an advantage.

Please apply to:

Screensafe plc
Screensafe House
66-71 High Street
Northton
NO1 2SS

Dear Mr Proto[1]

[2]

I am writing to apply for your job as a Trainee Windscreen Fitter[3]. I think I would enjoy this sort of work as I spend a lot of time helping family and friends to repair their cars[4]. I also go to car maintenance classes at Coltree Evening Centre[5].

I am enclosing my CV and hope to hear from you soon[6].

Yours sincerely,

---

8. Why is it an exciting field 'at the moment'? If the writer knows, it demonstrates up-to-date knowledge and to finish the sentence by briefly saying why would be a bonus.

This letter certainly gives a lot of useful information but could be improved nevertheless:

1. The writer has bothered to phone Screensafe and find out who to address the letter to. This shows initiative.

2. Always put a heading on your letter. It makes it easier to read and refer back to. If the organisation is advertising several vacancies it makes it easier for them to keep track of which letters belong where.

3. Tell the employer where you saw the advertisement.

4. This sentence is both good and bad. It comes across as enthusiastic and that's always good, but it also seems rather as if you're telling the employer what they can do for you rather than what you can do for

them. Perhaps it could be re-worded along the lines of, *'I have experience of stripping engines and replacing spare parts. I have helped re-spray an old Mini. I very much enjoy this type of work and go to Car...'*

5. Good to mention going to evening class, it shows real commitment.

6. Why not make this last sentence more sparky? *'I am enclosing my CV and hope you will feel that I have the qualities to make a good windscreen fitter.'*

HIGH MEADOWS HOUSING

Customer Services Clerk

We are looking for someone aged between 17 and 25 to fill this very important post. The job involves taking customer details, quoting prices and inputting data onto computer. The ability to deal tactfully with other companies and departments as well as with customers is vital.

Previous experience of this type of work would be an advantage.

Contact:

Mrs Mari Singh
Customer Services Manager
High Meadows Housing
High Meadows
Clydesfield
CL3 2DH

Dear Mrs Singh

Re: Customer Services Clerk

Your advertisement in this week's Recorder interests me very much. I am currently working as an Administrative Assistant for Briggs Ltd and feel that I have very relevant skills[1] for this vacancy. I am:

* experienced at dealing with customers

* familiar with Word and Excel

* used to liaising with other departments[2].

I am enclosing my CV and hope that you will give me an interview[3].

Yours sincerely

This is one way to lay out a covering letter – using bullet points again to highlight your skills. Here are some points you may have noticed about this letter:

1. This is a confident sentence which should keep the reader reading.

2. Good list of skills. The writer hasn't pointed out that s/he has no experience of giving quotes, it's simply implied by omission. That's fine because the advertisement only says 'previous experience would be an advantage' so they'll be willing to give someone training if necessary.

3. Although the list of skills is good, there is no mention of personal qualities. From the advertisement I am sure the postholder would need tact, good attention to detail, ability to keep calm under stress, good communication skills. The writer could have mentioned these even if they are already in the CV. Remember, if the employer gets a huge response they may not bother to read the CV if the covering letter is poor.

> *'People write some strange things in covering letters sometimes. One person wrote, 'I would really like this job (and that's the first time I've written that)'.'*

Quote from a personnel manager

SCHUMACHER LTD
are looking for

MACHINE/SETTER OPERATORS
to work as part of a team in our busy production department

You will need the ability to use simple tools to ensure that all our machinery is kept in good running order. Full training will be given although you must be capable of working on your own initiative once trained. The job involves heavy lifting. You must be literate and numerate and able to pass an aptitude text.

Hours 6 am-3 pm or 3 pm-10 pm

Contact:
The Personnel Department
Schumacher Ltd
Smyth Industrial Estate
Colmsworth
CO8 4MT

Dear Mr McGregor[1]

[2]

I am writting[3] about your job in the Recorder for a Machine Setter/
Operator[4].

Please find enclosed by CV. I am leaving school next month and think I
would be good at this sort of work[5].

I hope you will consider me for an interview[6].

Yours faithfully

Oops! I doubt if this person would get an interview if there was much
other choice.

1. This shows initiative, because the advertisement didn't show the name
   of the person to contact and the applicant has bothered to find out.

2. No heading!

3. Not good enough. The advertisement states that they're looking for
   someone who is literate. This person should have gone someone to
   check spelling before sending the letter off.

4. This sentence is poorly worded. It was the advertisement for a Setter/
   Operator, not a job for one.

5. Mmm, so the person thinks they'd be good for the job, but has
   failed to in any way try to convince the reader of the fact. S/he
   should have said why.

6. This sounds a bit grovelling. The sentence could be re-worded to
   sound more positive. Perhaps something like '*I am sure you will agree
   that I have potential for this type of work and hope you will grant me an
   interview.*'

7. Because the letter starts Dear Mr McGregor, it should end with
   Yours sincerely, not Yours faithfully.

DISPATCHER

Are you enthusiastic, neat and articulate? Do you have a good telephone manner? We are looking for someone to help in the daily picking and packing of our products for shipment all over the country. Full training will be given but previous dispatch experience would be helpful. Starting salary according to experience and age.

This position would suit a school leaver.

Write in the first instance to:

Mr Robert Chalmers
Dispatch Manager
Dyers of Lolswitch
Cowley Road
Lolswitch
LS4 4PP

Dear Mr Chalmers

Dispatcher vacancy

I am very interested in the above vacancy which was advertised in this week's *Lolswitch News*[1].

I am an enthusiastic[2] and energetic school leaver, punctual and reliable[3]. Although I have not done dispatch work before[4] I have worked in a shoe shop on Saturdays[5].

I am enclosing my CV which I hope[6] you will find interesting and hope[7] to hear from you soon.

Yours sincerely

A pretty good letter although it could be improved a little. Let's look at it point by point:

1. Often companies will want to know where you have learnt about a vacancy as it helps with their marketing.

2. It's useful to try to 'feed back' to the employer some of the words they've used in the advertisement. It helps them to feel at ease with your application.

3. This is good – four positive, personal qualities sold in one sentence!

4. Golden rule – don't highlight what you *haven't* done, let them find that out by reading your CV (or they may not bother to read it...). Emphasise instead what you *have* done.

5. It's fine to mention previous work experience but make the links. This sentence could read *'I have experience of working with others and controlling stock through my work as a Saturday Sales Assistant during my last two years at school.'*

6. This sentence sounds a bit feeble and could be much more punchy.

7. 'Hope' used twice in the same sentence. A final punchy sentence could be: *"I am very interested in working for your company which has a good reputation. I believe that my CV will show that I have many of the qualities you seek and look forward to hearing from you."*

> *'I advertised for a fairly high level post and was amazed at the poor presentation of some of the CVs and covering letters I received. One person had actually written on their covering letter 'I don't know what I can bring to the organisation'. Frankly, if he didn't know, why should I bother to try to find out!'*

Quote from an employer

Writing 'on spec'

Sometimes you may decide to write to an employer 'on spec' – where no job is advertised but you think you will write anyway and try your luck. This can be a very worthwhile approach. Chapter one gives further details of how to write these letters.

Sample covering letters

10 Gilbert Avenue
Anytown
Glos
GL2 3BL
01222 343536

Mr J. Brown
Corfield Industries
Unit 4, Anytown Industrial Estate
Anytown
Glos GL5 5PL

3 May 04

Dear Mr Brown

Clerical vacancies

I read in yesterday's 'Anytown Gazette' that Corfield Industries is extending it's operations in the near future and taking on additional staff. I am writing to ask if you would consider me for one of your clerical vacancies. I leave Anytown Regional College in June by which time I will have taken my BTEC in Business Studies.

I have enjoyed the Business Studies course very much, particularly the sections on finance and administration. My coursework grades have always been very good.

I have already put my learning to good use in my work placement with Jones Pharmaceuticals Ltd where I shadowed their Accounts Clerk. Through her excellent instruction I quickly learned how to use Excel (and have followed up this learning in my own time). Within a week I was making entries, dealing with simple enquiries and generally finding my way around.

An energetic person, I feel I can offer Corfield's not only my experience but my enthuasiasm, motivation and willingness to learn.

I will contact you within the next few days and hope to speak to you further then.

Yours sincerely

229 Main Street
Shireton
Cambs
SH4 4EE
01225 763421

Mrs Amez
Manager
Wonder Pizza Co
23 High Street
Shireton
SH 7 7OO

4 April 2004

Dear Mrs Amez

Vacancy for Chef

Your advertisement in today's Shireton Evening News interested me very
much because this is just the type of work I am looking for.

I am enclosing my CV for your information and from it you will see that I
have one year's experience as a waitress and one year working in the kitchen
for Giovanni's Restaurant whilst completing my education and City &
Guilds Catering. Giovanni's would, I feel sure, be very happy to provide a
reference for me.

In addition to my qualifications and experience I can also offer you my:

- enthusiasm
- ability to learn quickly
- willingness to continue training
- customer service skills
- ability to work in a busy kitchen
- knowledge of hygiene.

I hope that you will be interested in my application and that I will have an
opportunity to discuss this further with you at interview.

Yours sincerely

19 King's Street
Redfearn
Lanarkshire
RD3 3EE
01987 778865

Ms Reed
Personnel Manager
Grigg's Ltd
28 Dalton Street
Darmington
DA3 4TT

12 January 2004

Dear Ms Reed

Van Driver Vacancy

Please find attached my application form for the above vacancy which I saw advertised in today's 'Redfearn Weekly'.

As you will see, I have 18 months experience working for Jones Industries in Redfearn who would, I feel sure, be willing to provide a reference for me. During that time I made deliveries both locally and within a 100 mile radius. I also:

- had an unbroken attendance record

- was always punctual

- was accident free

- had a good reputation with both Jones' staff and customers.

I plan to move to the Darmington area within the next few weeks and am committed to living there. I am available for interview any day after the 27 January and hope to have an opportunity to speak to you then.

Yours sincerely

Beneficial Books plc
20 The Hythe
Colchester
CO1 1PP

30 February 2004

Dear Ms Chandler

Finance Clerk – Colchester Weekly News 28 January - Ref 27-090

Your advertisement in the Colchester Weekly News was of particular interest to me as I have just finished a two-year business studies course and took an additional unit in finance.

During the course I undertook a work placement with Jones engineering in their finance department. This was so successful that for the past year, in addition to my college course, I have worked for Jones' for ten hours per week.

My experience and education have given me an excellent grounding in the type of position you are advertising. My energy, commitment and integrity also make me a hardworking and reliable worker.

I would welcome an opportunity to discuss this appointment with you.

Yours sincerely,

Covering letter to support CV sent 'on spec' for part-time work

Purley Pizza Parlour
234 Main Road
Purley
PL1 3RF

4 February 2004

Dear Ms Perkins

Current/future vacancies

I am a final-year student at Purley Community College and am currently seeking part-time work in the catering business. I have just applied for a place on the City & Guilds Catering Course run at Action College and feel that the experience working with a reputable company such as your own would be invaluable.

In return I can offer you:

- a conscientious approach – I always meet deadlines and am very reliable

- good customer service skills – I have worked Saturdays for the past year in Progress Paper Shop

- willingness to learn

- flexibility.

As you can see from my CV, I have also taken three cookery courses at evening classes in my spare time and am currently attending an evening class on Business Skills.

I am enclosing my CV and would appreciate being considered should any vacancies arise.

Yours sincerely,

Chapter checklist

Remember that you should:

- always write a covering letter – they introduce your CV or application form. The exception for this is for college applications

- use good quality A4 paper

- use no more than one side of A4 paper

- make sure your hand writing can be read

- address the letter to the decision-maker

- remember to head the letter with the job title

- sign letters addressed to a named person with 'Yours sincerely'

- sign letters addressed to 'Dear Sir' or 'Dear Madam' with 'Yours faithfully'

- use the letter to highlight your strengths in relation to the post

- use the letter to provide any additional information not included in your CV or application form

- consider using bullet points if you want to get a lot of information across

- sound positive and confident, not grovelling and apologetic

- make sure the letter is articulate, pleasant to read, clean and perfect.

Index

W

More titles in the Student Helpbook series

NEW EDITION

Excel at Interviews 5th edition
Essential preparation for students and jobhunters.
£10.99   1902876 82 2

NEW EDITION

A Year Off … A Year On? 8th edition
Packed with all the information you need to make the most of your time out between courses or jobs.
£10.99   1 902876 86 5

NEW EDITION

Jobs and Careers after A Levels
and equivalent advanced level qualifications 8th edition
Opportunities for students leaving school or college at 18.
£10.99   1 902876 93 8

Student Life: A Survival Guide 3rd edition
Invaluable advice for anyone soon to begin university or college.
£10.99   1 902876 36 9

Careers with a Science Degree 3rd edition
Compulsory reading for anyone considering studying science at degree level.
£10.99   1 902876 66 0

Careers with an Arts Degree 3rd edition
Brimming with all the possibilities for anyone considering studying for an arts degree.
£10.99   1 902876 65 2

For further details please contact:

Customer services, Lifetime Careers Publishing, 7, Ascot Court, White Horse Business Park, Trowbridge, Wiltshire BA14 0XA.
Tel: 01225 716023; Fax: 01225 716025
Email: sales@lifetime-publishing.co.uk